Benjamin Franklin, Nilekaw Freeman, Jasper Richardson

A True and Faithful Account of the Island of Veritas

Together with the forms of their liturgy; and a full relation of the religious opinions

of the Veritasians, as delivered in several sermons just published in Veritas

Benjamin Franklin, Nilekaw Freeman, Jasper Richardson

A True and Faithful Account of the Island of Veritas

Together with the forms of their liturgy; and a full relation of the religious opinions of the Veritasians, as delivered in several sermons just published in Veritas

ISBN/EAN: 9783337315672

Printed in Europe, USA, Canada, Australia, Japan

Cover: Foto ©Lupo / pixelio.de

More available books at **www.hansebooks.com**

A

TRUE AND FAITHFUL ACCOUNT

OF THE

ISLAND of VERITAS;

TOGETHER WITH THE

FORMS OF THEIR LITURGY;

AND A FULL RELATION OF THE

RELIGIOUS OPINIONS

OF THE

VERITASIANS,

AS DELIVERED IN SEVERAL SERMONS

JUST PUBLISHED IN VERITAS.

LONDON:

Printed for C. STALKER, Stationer's-Court, Ludgate-Street.

PREFACE.

EVERY perſon, who publiſhes, is accountable to the world for the work he ſubmits to its peruſal.

The writer of the following hiſtory is my particular friend, and has generally ſent me a faithful relation of whatever he has diſcovered worthy of notice.

We were brought up together—our tempers diſpoſitions and purſuits were very ſimilar; and altho' the employment he is engaged in ſeparates us more frequently than we could wiſh, yet it tends to our mutual advantage; becauſe our reciprocal communications have always the improvement of the other for their end.

He ſailed the beginning of laſt year from Boſton, in America, upon an expedition to the ſouthward, and was to refreſh at Botany Bay,——I was very anxious for his ſafety, as I had not heard any thing of him for an unuſual length of time; but my fears were diſſipated by the arrival of the Lion, which brought me a packet, containing the following hiſtory, as well as a letter, of which this is an abſtract.

PREFACE.

My Dear Friend,

"A circumstance that made me fear I should never see you again, has been the means of bringing me acquainted with a most happy people."

(He then relates having been Ship-wrecked.)
"Some particulars of the Island we were cast upon I have enclosed——You are at liberty to publish them, because I am really in a state of uncertainty, whether the opinions you will find therein contained are false or true

"I feel myself almost converted to their way of thinking: but nevertheless I know not if the Veritasians are right, how it has happened that the Learned in England have permitted the world to remain so long in an error of such magnitude.

"Perhaps this history may occasion some controversy, if it should, do you be so good as to collect for me every thing pro and con that may be published before I return; when you and I will unbiassedly examine them, and endeavour to discover what is truth.

PREFACE.

"You may at all events sell my Yorkshire "estate, because I am determined, if it please "God to spare my life, to purchase a ship, "freight it with such things as may be useful "in Veritas, and get myself admitted as one "of its citizens,——could I prevail on you "and Mrs. Freeman to accompany me, my "pleasure would be greatly encreased, and "your good lady would be delighted with the "virtuous simplicity of this people.

"The Lion is getting under way—I have "only to add that I will not forget to send "you an account of Botany Bay as soon as "possible——I hope to be at home about "next Christmas."

Am, &c. &c.
Your sincere Friend,
JASPER RICHARDSON.

In conformity with the foregoing, I have published this history, and I beg the Learned of this nation to take the trouble of refuting whatever errors may be found in the opinions of the Veritasians, for from thence this benefit will be derived, that when my friend

Jasper goes next to the Island of Veritas, he will take with him such refutations, which, if they are convincing, will bring the Veritasians to a knowledge of the errors which they are in at present.

Either we or they are in an error, and which ever it is, mankind in general will be benefited in having this matter elucidated.

I shall be greatly obliged to all persons who may read this book, if they will favor me with their sentiments upon it, by letter addressed to me at the publishers, who am, with all truth,

Their very humble Servant,

Padderton,
Yorkshire.   NILEKAW FREEMAN,

To the Reviewers.

GENTLEMEN,

I am permitted to lay before you a short history of a nation, which my friend has discovered, inhabiting an island in the southern hemisphere.

PREFACE. vii.

I have given an abstract of his letter, which accompanied it, and I think I best answer his intention when I make the request, that you will critically and severely examine the opinions delivered in the discourses of the Veritasian priests.

The historical part is written, as you will perceive, by a person, not perhaps capable of producing any work sufficiently elegant for the publick's entertainment; but a simple statement of facts is as satisfactorily received from a sailor, whose truth is undoubted, as from the most perfect writer.

Ever since I have read his manuscript, I have felt myself very much interested in having these opinions thoroughly examined; and I doubt not but should any of our divines think it would be proper to endeavour to convert this people, that, by refuting and proving the falsity, and irrationality of the Veritasian doctrines, in a clear and argumentative manner, they would obtain their end; because all the Veritasians are remarkably open to conviction.

PREFACE.

Would you likewife, Gentlemen, in a fhort but clear manner point out their errors, it would greatly oblige
    Your very humble Servant,
            NILEKAW FREEMAN.

THE

HISTORY

OF THE

ISLAND OF VERITAS.

THE Iſland of Veritas is about three hundred miles long, and one hundred and fifty broad, the ſoil in general fertile, and the views picturesque:——Nature ſeems to have been partial in producing in this delightful ſpot, all the beauties which are admired in the reſt of the earth.

This Iſland received its name from an European, Jacobus Veritas;——he was a man of the ſtricteſt principles of honor, and his actions always marked the honeſt man; but diſpleaſed with the vices of the people amongſt whom he was born, and differing from them in his

B

opinions, he resolved to travel round the world, and acquaint himself with other nations, intending to settle wheresoever he should find mankind most virtuous and happy.

In the course of his voyages he landed upon the Island of Veritas, and from a superstitious custom of the people, was chosen their governor or king: Finding their manners simple, their tempers docile, their genious quick and inquisitive, he determined to put in force the scheme he had entertained from his youth; and on his *Death-bed* he had the satisfaction of knowing himself beloved by a nation, whose happiness was received from him.

He died much lamented, in the 91st year of his age, after a reign of 60 years:—his subjects have raised to his memory a very elegant monument, which, according to his will, has no other epitaph than the following.

HERE
WERE BURIED THE REMAINS
OF
JACOBUS VERITAS,
Ætatis Suæ, 91.
HE WAS A MAN
WHO BELIEVED
IN GOD,
AND ENDEAVOURED TO MAKE
THE GOODNESS
OF
THE ONE SUPRIME
KNOWN
TO ALL MANKIND.

Every act of his reign remains engraven on the hearts of the Veritafians, who fpeak of him with the highest veneration.

He planned their prefent form of government, which confifts of King, Lords and Commons, with all the principal regulations that are now in force.

Of the King of Parliament.

The crown is elective, and the following is their regulation for the election.

' As foon as the foul of a king fhall, by the pleafure
' of the Almighty God, be permitted to leave this earth,
' the lord in waiting fhall give notice thereof to the
' chancellor, who fhall forthwith fummons the parlia-

' ment to meet in the palace :—The commons shall then
' depute ten of their members to go with the chancel-
' lor to inspect the body,—when finding that the king did
' die a natural death, they shall make report thereof to the
' lords, who shall immediately proceed to elect, out of
' their own body, two persons to be returned to the com-
' mons, for them to chuse one of them to be king.

' Upon the choice being made, the lords and commons
' shall swear allegiance to their king; and shall take care
' that information be sent to every part of the realm, of
' whom they have elected.'

The privileges which the king enjoys are exactly the
same as those of the king of Great Britain, except where
otherwise ordered by particular laws.

It was considered by the founder of this government,
that perhaps, as the sovereign was to be chosen from the
lords, a conspiracy might sometime be formed to destroy
a future king, in order to promote a favorite of their own
body;—the law therefore provides, that ' In case the ex-
' amining committee from the commons, shall report
' that a malicious violence was the cause of the king's
' death, the chancellor shall then dissolve the parliament;
' a new one shall be chosen by the people, and from this
' new parliament shall a king be elected, who shall be
' enthroned by the chancellor.

' The king shall immediately direct the parliament to

' proceed to the election of the lords, and the chancellor
' shall inform the people of whom they have elected. *

Their title of lord is for a year, and signifies merely a lord of parliament.

The number of the lords is two hundred, but as they are only a separation from the commons, I will proceed to speak of the nature of electing the commons.

The whole Island is divided into one hundred divisions or counties,——each county is divided into one hundred parishes, and all persons who have attained the age of twenty-one years have a right to vote.

Every county has a sheriff, to whom the chancellor sends orders to return six members for his county. Upon receiving these orders, the sheriff directs the minister and church-wardens of each parish to collect the votes of their parishioners, for the appointment of six persons fit and proper to become members of parliament.

Having proceeded to the election, the minister and church-wardens make their return to the sheriff, and at the same time send to every parish in their county, a copy of the return so made by them.

---

* Although the crown is thus declared elective, yet the Veritasians have made it a point ever since the death of Jacobus, to chuse that person of his family for their king who would have been entitled to the crown had it been hereditary.

Upon receiving the parish returns, the sheriff calls up the number of the votes for the different candidates, and returns to the chancellor those six who have the majority; so likewise doth each parish receive from its officers an account of those persons upon whom the lot has fallen, whose names are painted on a particular part of the church, and remain there the whole year.

This election is annual, and the return is made to the chancellor the last week in the old year; the members meet the first monday in the second month of the new year, at the parliament house: when, after having sworn allegiance to the king, they proceed to the election of the two hundred lords of parliament, who are then presented to the king, for him to select a privy council of the number of sixty; but the whole body of lords meet in a separate house, and form a separate state from the commons.

No act of parliament has effect till it has gone through the same forms as in the parliament of Great Britain; but further, upon receiving the sanction of king, lords and commons, it is sent to a particular committee of the house of commons, which prepares an abstract of the same;——this abstract is returned to the commons for their approbation;—it is then carried to the lords, who, upon giving their assent, direct it to be printed and transmitted to every parish;—it is afterwards copied upon the walls of the church, and the printed abstract is preserved.

Of their Courts.

There is in each parish a court of twelve persons chosen annually by the rest of the parishioners, seven whereof make a court to transact business; they meet every fortnight for the determination of all causes of dispute that have arisen in the parish:——They reduce all the evidence to writing, which is sworn to by the parties; they give their sentence in writing, with the reasons for their verdict; and both the evidence and sentence is enrolled, and copies are kept by a parish register.

If through neglect of proper evidence, or through other causes, one party should have reason to think that the sentence of this court is unjust, he has a right to apply for relief to the sheriff of the county; who is then bound to send to every parish court under his jurisdiction, for them to nominate one of their members to meet him in the chief county town, on a day appointed; there to enquire into and determine the cause.

This court of one hundred, or as it is called, the Centum Court, when once chosen, lasts a twelvemonth from the time of its first sessions, and meets only once in three months, on a day appointed by itself, unless sooner called together by the sheriff.

This court, in case of any doubt, has a right to apply to the council for their advice, stating the facts to the council in writing, and confirming them, if necessary, by viva voce evidence.

All the courts strictly adhere to the letter of the written law, when there is any law applicable to the case; but otherwise, they give judgments in equity.

The persons who are chosen by the parish to compose the court of the twelve, exercise individually the power of the english justices of the peace.

The Island of Veritas is governed by four species of courts, at which, every person who knows himself wronged, may be successively heard, and may be sure of having his complaints redressed.

For, in the first instance, the magistrates or individuals of the twelve, have a power of redressing many grievances; and their sentence and conduct are examined into, by their aggregate body, when they next meet;—from this court an appeal lies to the centum;—from thence to the council;—and from the council to the parliament:——But in order to prevent unnecessary and troublesome appeals, every court that confirms the former sentence, has the power of doubling the penalty, which it is expected to do, unless there appears to have been sufficient cause to justify the appeal.

Of the Officers of State.

All officers of state are appointed by the king, except the chancellor,——the sheriff,——and the judges.

The Chancellor is the firſt officer of the realm; his appointment is for life, and he has a fixed ſalary, paid by the treaſury: He is made by the lords and commons giving their aſſent to the recommendation of the king.

He is a privy councellor and prolocutor of the lords; and ſits at the right hand of the throne when the privy council are examining the merits of any appeal.

He is the general guardian of all infants, idiots and lunatics: To him is intruſted thoſe extraordinary powers of applying the force of government, to afford that remedy for any ill which could not be given if the injured perſon is obliged to wait for the courſe of the laws: But as ſuch a power might be ſometimes uſed to the injury of ſociety, it was ! ought neceſſary by Jacobus that it ſhould be intruſted to ſome perſon who might be amenable to the cenſure of the parliament: Yet as from this the king is exempt, upon our principle that a king can do no wrong, ſo on that account the chancellor is inveſted with this power, which in many countries belongs ſolely to the ſovereign.

The public ſeals are given to the cuſtody of the chancellor, but he is not obliged to put the ſeal to any thing he thinks may be injurious to the king, until he has received the direct poſitive orders of the privy council of the lords and of the commons.

C

He has a court compofed of himfelf and the judges, which receives annually a regifter of all the caufes that have been tried by any of the courts of juftice, with their judgments; and in cafe that a charge of willful mifconduct brought againft any of the magiftrates be proved, this court, with the confent of the privy council fines the offender.

Of the Sheriff.

The next officer in rank and confequence in the ftate is the Sherifh of a county.

Upon the death of a fheriff, the court of the one hundred is fummoned by the chancellor, to return to the king three perfons born in the county, who are fit and proper to fill this office.—— Of thefe the king chufes whom he moft approves.——This office is for three years certain; after which time he is removable either by the will of the king, or by petition from the centum, which petition the king muft grant.

To this officer are fent the writs for the election of the members of parliament; and by him is the return made. He has a feat at the head of the hundred court.—To him the confirming the fentences of the court is intrufted, and he has a right to order once, a re-examination of any caufe which appears doubtful to him.

He has alfo power to command the parifh courts to enquire into particular abufes, and to make their report to him.

Of the Judges.

The four and twenty judges are appointed by the parliament, at the recommendation of the king, and they hold their offices for the life of the king; their busineſs is to ſuperintend the framing of laws, taking care that they are ſimple, clear and neceſſary: They alſo explain to the houſes of parliament the meaning and connexion of any of the laws; which explanation, if approved of by the parliament and thought neceſſary, is recorded and added to the former law. They ſit in the houſe of lords, but never give any vote: And have certain ſalaries, payable by the treaſury.

The reſt of the officers of ſtate are appointed by the king, are removable by him whenever he pleaſes, and from him they receive their ſalaries: Two of his principal ſecretaries have ſeats ex officio in the houſe of commons.

Of the Revenue.

The expences of government are borne by the parliament, who raiſe the ſupplies neceſſary thereto in the moſt ſimple manner poſſible.

There is neither cuſtom, exciſe, or duty of any kind; for they think that ſuch are hurtful to a ſtate, by rendering it neceſſary to be at the expence of hiring people to collect them; which in the firſt inſtance occaſions a burthen; and alſo, that it is laying a temptation in the way of the fraudulent to injure the honeſt and conſcientious: Of this they ſay they are convinced, by the hiſtories of other nations.

Their method of levying the neceffary fupplies is as follows.——The king fends to the commons, to defire them to meet him in the houfe of lords; he there briefly ftates the computed expences of the current year, and leaves them all the vouchers of the application of the laft fupplies.————The commons then retire to their own houfe, and one of the fecretaries of ftate gives them copies of the vouchers.

The lords and commons feparately prepare their opinions of what fum of money ought to be raifed by each county; thefe they fend to each other.——If there is any difference, the commons defire a conferrence with the lords; at this conferrence five lords are elected by the commons, and five of the commons by the lords, who finally determine the quotas to be raifed; and in cafe of an equal divifion on any contefted point, the king decides.

When all is agreed and fettled, the commons prepare a bill for levying the neceffary revenue; and when the bill is paffed, the chancellor, by the king's order, fends writs to the fheriffs, requiring each of them to call together his court of the one hundred, to lay before it the act of parliament, and to require it to raife the neceffaries.——This court proportions the fum required according to the abilities of its refpective conftituent parifhes, which are bound to fend their quota within a certain time to the fheriff, who tranfmits them to the treafury.

Every officer under goverment has a certain salary, no perquisites being allowed; and failure in integrity is punished in every department with the utmost severity.

Of their Laws.

Their code of laws is very simple.

Their parish courts have power of ordering restitution to be made for every wrong, but if the convicted party thinks himself unjustly sentenced, he may, within ten days, appeal to the sheriff for a further examination by the centum court, which may either reverse the sentence of the parish court, or order its being put into immediate execution: If the party does not appeal within the limited time, the parish courts have power to proceed to execution.

The Veritasians punish no offence with death; they say they have no right to take away life, except in self-defence.

Two benefits they think are desirable from laws;——the correction and prevention of wrongs.———Sanguinary laws are known to fail.

Murder they esteem the most atrocious crime, yet they believe they should not be justified in taking the life of the murderer; because, as the offence is against God, immediate human punishment may prevent the effect of repentance, and a soul may thereby be destroyed.

But as the murderer cannot expect favor from society, they therefore condemn him to perpetual solitary imprisonment; where, provided with good books, he is left to endeavour to appease his God, for a wrong he can never reinstate to man.———He has food sufficient to keep him alive, brought to him once a day, by the goaler, who is forbidden ever to speak to him.

Other crimes are punished with temporary imprisonment, the time being proportioned to the offence:— Every man in prison is kept separate and solitary; nor has he an opportunity of seeing any body but the person who brings his food.

The name of every person who is sent to prison, is published in his parish church, on the sunday next after his commitment, with the nature of the offence and the sentence passed upon him.

Of Change of Property.

In the descent of property among the Veritasians, the nearest relations, whether male or female; or of the whole or half blood, take possession of all property in equal shares, except where otherwise ordered by particular laws.

Their wills require few formalities, because if there be a widow and children, she has a life interest in half the property, the rest being equally divided among the children; and at her death, her share becomes the equal property of all the children; nor can a will alter this succession: Where there are no children, a man may leave one half of his property to whomsoever he pleases; the other being his widows, if he leaves one; but this will muſt be atteſted by three witneſſes.

Their conveyance of real eſtates is made by actual livery of ſeizen, which is regiſtered in the hundred court.

The foregoing are the heads of their government and laws, and ſo ſimple is the adminiſtration of juſtice, and ſo well acquainted are all the Veritaſians with the laws, that the offences which are brought before the courts, are as few as can be ſuppoſed; indeed to the excellent regulations of their reſpective pariſhes, are to be attributed their happineſs and virtue.

Mentioning their pariſhes, I am led to take notice of their clergy and their ſchools.

The living of each pariſh is worth about two hundred and fifty pounds a year of our money; this ſum is raiſed by government, with the other expences, and the pariſh officers deduct it from the account they ſend to the ſheriff.——— This is divided into two parts £150 for a miniſter, and £100 for a curate; but both are obliged to reſidence; nor can one clergyman hold two livings. Theſe clergy are elected annually by the pariſh; when they are returned to ſix officers, called inſpectors of the clergy, who go a circuit every year through different diviſions, to inſpect and make their reports to the chancellor.—But when once a clergyman is elected, he cannot be turned out, nor can another be elec'ed without sufficient reason being given to the infpectors, who, before they admit the new one, muſt receive the chancellor's affent.

As the clergy enter into the profeſſion with the firm determination of doing their duty, fo to them is intruſted the education of all the youth in the pariſh.———They fuperintend the fchools, and examine that parents teach their children to read their native tongue; they take care that there be always a fupply of proper books provided at the expence of the pariſh, for the ufe of the children; endeavouring to procure fuch books as may give them a juſt knowledge of their own nature, thereby enabling them properly to glorify their creator.*

There are in Veritas ten public fchools or colleges, where languages, arts and fciences may be acquired, and a finiſhed education received.——Thefe are attended with fome expence to thofe perfons who fend their children to them; but the regulations are fo excellent, that in them almoſt all the chief people of the nation have fome part of their education, although the parents themfelves are the chief inſtructors of their children.

In thefe fchools they who intend to be clergymen finiſh their education and receive a certificate of being properly qualified for the duties of their profeſſion, but an immoral man will never be able to

---

* Every pariſh alfo has particular regulations for the employment of its poor—fo that in Veritas no man ever complains of being unable to find work.

gain it.———They are very particular in enquiring into the virtue of their clergy, becaufe it is their opinion that the fociety which admits immoral men into the profeffor-fhip of its religion, muft be in a very rotten ftate.

The enquiry whether a man is a virtuous citizen? is with them a matter of great concern; and he who wilfully violates the laws of God and virtue, is fure to meet the cenfure of the twelve, and to be fent into temporary confinement.

Every perfon is brought up to fome bufinefs or employment; for the Veritafians believe that an idle man can hardly fail of being vicious.

They trade with the utmoft integrity, and their word is at all times as facred as a bond.——— They feem exceffively fond of traffick, but feldom venture beyond their capital:—They are very frugal and induftrious, therefore failures are very rare with them; if, however, fuch by accident fhould happen, the creditors of the unfortunate meet together and examine his books, and if they find it has been through unavoidable loffes, they affift in putting him into trade again; but if avarice, or extravagance have been the caufe of his error, they deliver him to the twelve for their examination, who, if they think proper, order him into confinement.

They are a lively cheerful people, fond of meetings where the old and young can mix together, and where the innocent pleasures of youth are recalled to their minds, by the sight of the same joys in their children.— They condemn the unnatural austerities, which are practised by many nations; they declare that God is good; that he is pleased when his creatures are happy, and that all his appointments are wise: But neverthelefs, they acknowledge that man does sometimes commit actions which are very wrong; yet, this they say, proceeds solely from his being ignorant of what is right.—When told, that some people contend that man is naturally vicious, they deny it, and affert, that the errors which other nations give into cannot be attributed to nature, for they are in fact unnatural, as tending to defeat the intentions of God.

It appears extraordinary to them, when they read of men devoting all their time to amafs gold and jewels, in order that it may be faid, they die worth fo much. Human nature cannot receive any advantage from them after death; yet, to obtain riches, many men are guilty of practices which make them run the greateft hazard of being miserable in the future ftate; for avarice and vanity do not leave them any time to think of what may be their lot hereafter.

Another thing, which appears aftonifhing to them, is, that men and women in fome parts of the world live together merely for the gratification of their appetites; and, that many women gain their living by common proftitution.

God, they fay, made man and woman, that they fhould live together, but ordained, that by their union the fpecies fhould be continued.——Connexions therefore, where no iffue is defired, cannot be called natural; indeed they are intirely deftructive of the end intended.

Such never happen with them; they follow the dictates of regulated nature, and turn all their paffions to a proper and happy courfe. They inftruct their children in the knowledge of every thing; and particularly in the confequence of making a proper connexion in order to their future happinefs, to which, virtue is the only guide.

The neceffaries of life being all they wifh, are eafily procured: And the Veritafians teach their children at an early period to employ themfelves ufefully. Thus, taking away the motives that actuate many nations to delay matrimonial connexions,—their youth foon marry, for the parents have feldom occafion to diffent, becaufe virtue is the chief fortune that is required both by the parents and children. We afked whether their children had not too early a defire for marriage? They faid, it was very feldom the cafe, and even when it was, that it could be turned to the greateft advantage if the child had been properly educated;—for inftance, if a fon fhould fancy himfelf in love, they generally approved of the perfon upon whom he had fet his affections, extolled her as much as he could wifh,—and then pointing out to him some branches of learning, of which he still remained ignorant,—they asked him whether he could think that he was intitled to marry such a virtuous and accomplished woman ?——Advised him to study in all things to oblige her, to gain her affections, and to prove himself worthy of her; but before he should venture to ask a return of her love, to acquaint himself with those parts of education of which he was ignorant, and assured him that, whenever he should find himself deserving of her, all his parents interest should be joined with his, in order that his wishes might be gratified.

What surprizes them most is, that the people who call themselves christians, who say that the most high God took upon himself our form, suffered death upon the cross, offered up himself a sacrifice to himself for the sins of the world; and who left behind him precepts commanding every virtue:——That these should be the people who most generally, according to history, give themselves up to the errors of avarice and licentious gratifications.

The Veritasians are strictly virtuous, and are truly religious, although their opinions differ from ours.——They meet in prayer every night and morning in their own families; for since God has not forbid their addressing him, they assert that they should be wrong in neglecting to exercise this great privilege of man, even if God would not always hear them; but as they are satisfied that he always will hear the prayers of the humble, they esteem the honor of being permitted to call upon him as the most invaluable of any they enjoy.

Their form of prayer bears a great similitude to ours, and was clearly taken from it by Jacobus; there are some trifling alterations which render it seemingly more connected, and other grand alterations arising from their creed.* I here subjoin their form of public service, and shall afterwards convey their religious sentiments through the assistance of some sermons, which are in the highest estimation in Veritas.

MORNING SERVICE.

Prayer to be used by all Persons upon entering the Church.

O Almighty and ever merciful God! I beseech thee to cleanse my heart from all impurities, and let thy holy spirit enable me to render unto thee, a faithful and acceptable service. Amen.

---

* I told one of their clergy that I thought they had spoiled their first psalm, [our 95th] by altering the beautiful eastern mode of expression; and that the harmony of their numbers was no ways equal to the translation, used by the church of England; it might be so, he said, but he was satisfied it was more agreeable to reason; and he could not conceive the benefit to be expected from worshiping God in metaphor.

The Minister shall address the People as follows.

O Come, let us worship the lord: let us heartily rejoice in the strength of our salvation.

Let us come before his presence with thanksgiving: and shew ourselves devoted unto him.

For the lord is a great god: and a great king over all creation.

The sea is his, and he made it: his power prepared the dry land.

O come, let us worship, and fall down: and kneel before the lord our maker.

For he is the lord our god: and we ought always to offer unto him our unfeigned thanksgivings.

To day if you will render him acceptable service, harden not your hearts: as we read, that the Jews did in the provocation and in the day of temptation in the wilderness; when, as their historians inform us, they tempted him and saw his greatness.

Forty years long did they wander in the wilderness; and proved that they were a people who did err in their hearts, for they did not know his ways.

Yet, he bore with their sins; and had mercy on their transgressions:

And permitted them to enter the land which, according to the bible, was flowing with milk and honey.

Let us Praise God.

Glory be to thee; O thou most highest!

The People shall say.

May thy name be blessed, thy ways be known, and thy Will be performed by all mankind.—Blessed be thy name, O God, for ever and ever. Amen.

The Minister shall exhort the people as follows.

If we say that we have no sin, we deceive ourselves, and the truth is not in us; but if we confess our sins, and sincerely repent, God is merciful and will forgive us our sins, and will cleanse us from all unrighteousness.

DEARLY beloved brethren, the scripture moveth us in sundry places to acknowledge and confess our manifold sins and wickedness, and it is evident to our reason that we should not dissemble, nor cloak them before the face of almighty God, who knoweth all the secrets of our hearts, but that we should confess them, with an humble, lowly, penitent and obedient heart; to the end that we may obtain forgiveness of the same, by his infinite goodness and mercy.—And although we ought at all times humbly to acknowledge our sins before God, yet ought we most chiefly to do, when we assemble and meet together, to render thanks for the great benefits we have received from him, to set forth his most worthy praise and to ask those things which are requisite and necessary, as well for the body as the soul.—Wherefore I pray and beseech you, as many as are here present, to accompany me with a pure heart and humble voice unto the throne of the heavenly grace.

ALMIGHTY and moſt merciful father, We have erred and ſtrayed from thy ways, We have followed too much the deſires of our own hearts.——We have offended againſt thy holy laws; We have left undone thoſe things which we ought to have done; and we have too often done thoſe things which we ought not to have done.--But do thou, O Lord! have mercy upon us repenting ſinners.—Spare thou them, O God, which confeſs and repent of their faults.——Reſtore thou them that are penitent—according to the aſſurances given to mankind by jeſus chriſt.—— And grant, O moſt merciful father!—that thy holy ſpirit may evermore aſſiſt us—in leading godly, righteous and ſober lives.—— To thy glory.——Amen.

The miniſter ſhall then make this declaration.

ALMIGHTY God! the creator of all things, deſireth not the death of a ſinner, but would rather that he ſhould turn from his wickedneſs.——And we may be aſſured, that the mercy of the moſt high will be extended to all thoſe who truly repent of their former ſins, and endeavour, with an humble and a contrite ſpirit, to paſs the reſt of their days in holineſs and virtue.

Let us therefore beſeech almighty God, to grant us true repentance and an holy ſpirit, that thoſe things may pleaſe him which we do at this preſent, and that the reſt of our lives hereafter may be pure and holy, according to the example ſet us of a perfect life by jeſus chriſt, in whoſe moſt comprehenſive form of prayer let us call upon the eternal for his bleſſing.

The Minifter and the Congregation kneeling fhall filently and devoutly offer up the Prayer.

OUR father, who art in heaven, hallowed be thy name. Thy kingdom come. Thy will be done on earth, as it is in heaven. Give us this day our daily bread. And forgive us our trefpaffes, as we forgive them that trefpafs againſt us. And lead us not into temptation; but deliver us from evil: For thine is the kingdom, and the power, and the glory, for ever and ever. Amen.

Minifter.

O Lord, open thou our lips;

People.

And our mouth fhall fhew forth thy praife.

Minifter.

O God, be pleafed to fave us.

People.

O Lord, we befeech thee to hear us.

Here follows the Litany.

OGod, the creator of the univerfe: have mercy upon us, accept our prayers, affift our infirmities, and forgive us our fins.

We befeech thee to hear us, good Lord.

Remember not our offences, nor the offences of our fore-fathers; neither take thou vengeance of our fins: fpare us good Lord; fpare thy people, and be not angry with us for ever.

Spare us good Lord.

From all evil and mischief, from sin, and from thy heavy displeasure.

Good Lord deliver us.

From all blindness of heart: from pride, vain-glory and hypocrisy; from envy, hatred, and malice; and all uncharitableness.

Good Lord deliver us.

From lightning and tempest: from plague, pestilence, and famine; from battle and murder, and from sudden death.

Good Lord deliver us.

From all sedition and conspiracies: from ignorance of our nature, and of our duty towards thee; and from contempt of those laws which our reason informs us are declaratory of thy will.

Good Lord deliver us.

In all time of our tribulation: in all time of our wealth; in the hour of death, and in the day when we shall be in thy presence to receive thy judgment upon our actions.

Good Lord deliver us.

We sinners do beseech thee to hear us, O Lord God; and that it may please thee to make thy ways known to all mankind.

We beseech thee to hear us, good Lord.

That it may pleafe thee to blefs our fovereign and his family, ſtrengthening them in the true knowledge of thee.

We befeech thee to hear us, good Lord.

That it may pleafe thee to endue the council, parliament, and all the other courts, with wifdom, underſtanding and the love of juſtice;

We befeech thee to hear us, good Lord.

That it may pleafe thee to blefs and keep our magiſtrates and all perfons who are in office; and to give them grace to execute their truſts with fidelity;

We befeech the to hear us, good Lord.

That it may pleafe thee to illuminate all the teachers of religion with true knowledge and underſtanding; and that both by their preaching and living they may contribute to thy glory, and to the confequent happinefs of this nation;

We befeech thee to hear us, good Lord.

That it may pleafe thee to give to all nations, unity, peace, and concord;

We befeech thee to hear us, good Lord.

That it may pleafe thee to blefs and keep all thy people;

We befeech thee to hear us, good Lord.

That it may pleaſe thee to give us an heart to love ~~husband~~ thee, and diligently to live after thy commandments;

We beſeech thee to hear us, good Lord.

That it may pleaſe thee to preſerve us from all bigotry and ſuperſtition; and to bring into the way of truth all ſuch as are deceived;

We beſeech thee to hear us, good Lord,

That it may pleaſe thee to comfort and help all ſuch as are in danger, neceſſity, or tribulation;

We beſeech thee to hear us, good Lord.

That it may pleaſe thee to preſerve all that travel by land or by water, all women labouring with child, all ſick perſons and young children, and to ſhew thy pity upon all priſoners and captives;

We beſeech thee to hear us, good Lord.

That it may pleaſe thee to defend and provide for the fatherleſs children and widows, and all that are deſolate and oppreſſed;

We beſeech thee to hear us, good Lord.

That it may pleaſe thee to have mercy upon all men;

We beſeech thee to hear us, good Lord.

That it may pleaſe thee to give and preſerve to our uſe, the kindly fruits of the earth, ſo that in due time we may enjoy them;

We beſeech thee to hear us, good Lord.

That it may please thee to give us true repentance; to forgive us all our sins, negligences, and ignorances, and to endue us with the grace of thy holy spirit, to amend our lives, and to pafs our days in friendship, charity, and brotherly love with all men; whereby, we best prove the sincerity of our devotions to thee, who art the God of mercy, and who wisheth the happiness of all thy creatures;

We beseech thee to hear us, good Lord.

We beseech thee, O father of mercies to hear our prayers; and of thy goodness to keep from us those things we at any time may afk which will be hurtful unto us, and vouchsafe to give us those good things which will be necessary to our welfare, even should our ignorance prevent us from afking them. Amen.

We beseech thee to hear us, good Lord.

Let us Pray.

O God, merciful father, who despisest not the fighing of a contrite heart, nor the desire of such as be sorrowful, mercifully assist our prayers that we make before thee, in all our troubles and adversities whensoever they oppress us: and graciously hear us that those evils which threaten us, and which we have justly merited, may, by thy providence, be averted; that we thy servants being hurt by no persecution, may pafs our time in rest and quietness, and may glorify thee for thy goodnefs in permitting mankind, through Jefus Chrift, to know thee, the one God, the creator of all things. Amen.

O God, we have heard with our ears; and we ourfelves have known the greatnefs of thy majefty, of thy mercy, and of thy power:

We befeech thee therefore gracioufly to look upon our afflictions.

Pitifully to behold the forrows of our hearts.

Mercifully to forgive the fins of thy people.

Favorably with mercy to hear our prayers.

O God, let thy mercy be fhewed unto us,

For we do put our truft in thee.

Let us Pray.

WE humbly befeech thee, O Father, mercifully to look upon our infirmities; and for the glory of thy name, turn from us all thofe evils that we moft righteoufly have deferved: and grant that, in all our troubles, we may put our whole truft and confidence in thee, and evermore ferve thee in holinefs and purenefs of living, to thy honor and glory. Amen.

O Almighty God, who hast given us grace at this time, with one accord, to make our common supplications unto thee: fulfil now, O Lord, the desires and petitions of thy servants, as may be most expedient for them, granting them in this world the knowledge of thy truth; and, when thou shalt be pleased to call them hence, giving them to know that their lives had been passed in conformity with thy will; that their souls will be accepted by thee, and admitted to that highest of blessings, the more perfect knowledge of the glory of their God. Amen.

May the love of God be with us all evermore. Amen.

End of the Litany.

The following address to the deity, to be offered up by the minister aloud, the people following him silently.

WE praise thee O God! we acknowledge thee to be the Lord.
All the earth doth worship thee, the father everlasting!
'Tis thee! creation doth adore.
The heavens and all the powers therein.
To thee! they offer up their praise.
To thee! their father and their God!
Holy! holy! holy! Lord God of sabaoth!
Heaven and earth, are full of the majesty of thy glory,

We praise thee, O God! we thank thee for thy mercy,
In sending upon earth the blessed Jesus, to dispel the darkness of the idolatrous world!
Without this mercy, we should have remained in ignorance of thee;
The only God!
And should have still worshipped the idols of the heathens:
But thy mercy is unbounded! and thy goodness without end.
Vouchsafe, O Lord! to keep us this day without sin:
That we may worthily magnify thy holy name.
Make us to be numbered with thy saints in glory everlasting.
O Lord, save thy people and bless them.
Govern them, and lift them up for ever.
O Lord have mercy upon us, have mercy upon us.
O Lord let thy mercy lighten upon us, as our trust is in thee.
O Lord in thee have I trusted, let me never be confounded.

Then the Minister shall say

Let us thank God for his mercies, and let us pray to Almighty God that he will give us a due understanding of the scriptures.

Minister.

O Almighty and omniscient God, whose goodness exceedeth the utmost stretch of human abilities; we thank thee for all thy mercies, more especially for the faculty of reason, whereby we are distinguished from and exalted above the rest of thy creatures upon earth: continue, we pray thee, thy favor unto us, and let thy holy spirit move us to a due exercise of our rational powers, that we may know, and fear, and love thee, the only God: keep us from all bigotry and superstition, which ever have a tendency to diminish thy glory; and empower us in all temptations to look up to thee with confidence and trust.——And now, O Lord, we beseech thee to enlighten us with thy wisdom, that as we are going to read a portion of the scriptures, esteemed by many nations thine inspired work, we may, through thy blessing, be able to know what is necessary for fulfilling thy will; and, by the examples there introduced, may see that thy providence is always watchful over all thy works, and that, (as thy unalterable goodness can never change) thou, having from the first made man a free agent, hast not destroyed that free agency, not even in preventing the introduction of errors into these respected writings.—— Enable us therefore, we humbly intreat thee, to discover those errors and to receive profit from them, through convincing ourselves how liable human nature is to be deceived by the arts of the designing or superstitious.——We, thy servants, acknowledge thy perfection and thy immutability.——We know that we are bound to do thy will in all things.—— We pray thee to acquaint us with it, and to give us grace to perform it. Amen.

People.

We beseech thee, to grant this petition, O thou most mighty.

Then shall the Minister read the appointed Lessons in the Bible and Testament.

Afterwards let the Minister deliver a discourse adapted to the lessons, explaining what is necessary, and pointing out any apparent error in the reading; assuring his Auditors that God never made any revelation to mankind that he did not wish them to understand, and that those things which are not satisfactory to our reason, cannot be the revelations of omniscience.—— Let him enlarge upon the duties that were taught and inculcated by Jesus Christ; let him teach the greatness and goodness of God, and explain the real consequence of man in the general system of creation, and let him finish his sermon with this psalm:

O Be joyful in the Lord, all ye lands: serve the Lord with gladness, and come before his presence with rejoicing.

Be ye sure that the Lord he is God; that it is he who hath made us, and not we ourselves.

O come into his gates with thankfgivings, and into his courts with praife: be thankful unto him, and fpeak good of his name.

For the Lord is gracious, his mercy is everlafting, and his truth endureth from generation to generation.

Here follows the Belief, to be pronounced aloud by all.

I Believe in God, the father almighty, maker of heaven and earth: And of all things vifible and invifible. I believe that his power and wifdom are unbounded; that he is, from all eternity, a fole felfexiftent God, and that his duration is without end.

I believe that he made man, the moft perfect creature upon earth; giving him reafon that he might difcover his own nature and might ferve his God in righteoufnefs and holinefs of life: and I believe that God made man a free agent and left him to the free exercife of his powers.

I believe that the earth is a fmall orb, (in comparifon with the reft of creation) revolving round the fun along with other orbs forming one fyftem; and which, although of immenfe extent, occupies but as a point in the incomprehenfibility of fpace.

I believe that God made the ftars, whofe diftance from us is fo great as to be immeafurable.---And perceiving that on earth he has done nothing in vain: I do not doubt but the ftars are fyftems of worlds filled with creatures who partake of the bounty of their God.

I believe that creation was an act of the goodnefs of God, and therefore that every thing neceffary to the happinefs of his creatures was provided for them; and that whatever unhappinefs is met with in the world has arifen through the mifufe of the bounties of God.

I believe that God had compaffion upon the errors and ignorances of mankind, who, in a courfe of years, had forgotten their maker and worfhiped the works of their own hands. I believe that his holy fpirit permitted Jefus Chrift to have an enlightened idea of his attributes, and that Chrift contemning the world when put in competition with the honor of the great creator, fuffered the cruel death of the crofs with conftancy, in proof of the truth of his doctrines.

I believe in a future ftate, when the almighty will be pleafed to make himfelf known to thofe creatures who have rendered themfelves worthy of that greateft of bleffings; and I firmly believe that the virtuous will be rewarded with everlafting happinefs.

N. B. It is to be remarked of every Belief, that, as it is a declaration in the prefence of God, before the congregation, of what a perfon fays he *believes*, if he either doubts or does not underftand any parts of the belief he utters, fo as not to feel a perfect conviction, it is the higheft perjury a man can be guilty of.——If there is any thing in the above belief incomprehenfible to any one, let him pafs it by, and let no man prefume to declare his belief in what he has doubts of.——God requires no fet form of words, the heart alone he judges of, and the fimple and the contrite fpirit will he not defpife.

Prayer by the Minister.

GRANT we beseech thee, Almighty God, that thy holy spirit may urge us to a continuance in doing good works, and may assist us in all our dangers and tribulations.——Strengthen our faith in thee, and increase our knowledge of thee.——Make us to prove ourselves worthy the exalted station to which thou hast called us, by ever conducting ourselves with humility towards thee, and with love to our fellow creatures.—— Make us to know that thy goodness can have no other design in creation than of dispensing happiness; and that if any other result takes place it is not agreeable to thee, but that it arises from the perverseness of thy creatures, to whom thou hast permitted the freedom of chusing what is right or following what is wrong.

Thy mercy shines conspicuous in all things here on earth: And thy greatness in the immense, though regular systems of worlds which thy goodness has permitted the senses of man to perceive, suspended in the regions of space, in harmony fulfilling thy will.

Teach us to know our duty towards thee;—to perform thy will in all thy things;—to pass our lives subservient to the dictates of reason.——Make us to be truly sensible of thy mercies, more especially of the blessings we enjoy, through the merits of Jesus Christ, of being the worshipers of thee, the true God, instead of remaining in the ignorant worship of idols.

Make us, in all our actions, to prove ourselves worthy of this transcendent goodness, and assist us in conducting ourselves in such a manner as may not be displeasing to thee, derogatory to thy greatness, or unworthy of creatures to whom thou hast permitted a knowledge of thy attributes.

To thee, O Lord, we address ourselves, who knowest the infirmities of man.———We beseech thee to have compassion upon us who are continually liable to forget our God, through attending too much to the solicitations of temporal concerns; send down thy blessings upon us, who humbly seek thee, and comfort us, in all our troubles, with the consciousness that thy assistance is not far from us.——Let love and unanimity pervade the whole of thy people; let thy protection be given to all sorts and conditions of men: and inspire us all with such a sense of our duty towards thee, that we may evermore regulate our actions to thy glory.

Accept, O most mighty and most perfect being, the services which we thy servants do, in this thy day, endeavour to render unto thee; and grant, that we may continue, daily, to increase in grace, until it shall please thee to call us from our earthly body to that blessed immortality, which our souls most fervently hope for.

To thee, and to thy name be all honor and glory, world without end. Amen.

End of the Morning Service.

EVENING SERVICE.

Prayer:

PREVENT us, O Lord, in all our doings with thy moſt gracious favor, and further us with thy continual help; that in all our works begun, continued and ended in thee, we may glorify thy holy name; and finally, by thy mercy obtain everlaſting life, according to the aſſurances delivered to us, by Jeſus Chriſt. Amen.

Miniſter.

O GIVE thanks unto the Lord, for he his gracious, and his mercy endureth for ever.

O let your ſongs be of him, and praiſe him, and let your talking be of all his wondrous works.

Yet who can expreſs the noble acts of the Lord! or ſhew forth all his praiſe!

Seek the Lord, O ye people! rejoice in his holy name; let the heart of thoſe who ſeek the Lord rejoice.

For he is the Lord our God; and his judgments are in all the world.

Thanksgiving.

ALMIGHTY God, father of all mercies, we, thine unworthy servants, do give thee most humble and hearty thanks for all thy goodness, and loving kindness to us and all men.

We bless thee for our creation, preservation, and all the blessings of this life; but above all for thine inestimable love, in suffering the blessed Jesus to declare to mankind the truths of thy greatness and power; thus giving us the means of grace, whereby we hope for glory.——And we beseech thee, give us that due sense of all thy mercies, that our hearts may be unfeignedly thankful, and that we may shew forth thy praise, not only with our lips, but in our lives, by giving up ourselves to thy service, and by walking before thee in holiness and righteousness all our days, through the instructions left us by Jesus Christ, in whose most perfect form of words we offer up our humble petitions.

The Minister and Congregation shall silently pray.

OUR father, which art in heaven, hallowed be thy name. Thy kingdom come. Thy will be done on earth, as it is in heaven. Give us this day our daily bread. And forgive us our trespasses, as we forgive them that trespass against us. And lead us not into temptation; but deliver us from evil: For thine is the kingdom, and the power, and the glory, for ever and ever. Amen.

Minister.

DEARLY beloved brethren.—In the bible, and in the 20th chapter of Exodus, we find a set of commandments, said to have been delivered by the almighty to Moses.

Their beautiful, yet majestic simplicity, proves them to have been written by one who felt the greatness of God, and our reason assents to their propriety.——In their due observance all religion and morality consists. I will therefore read part of them to you; and let us, after each commandment, offer unto the Almighty a prayer, that he will have mercy upon us, and incline our hearts to keep these laws.

COMMANDMENTS.

I. Thou shalt have none other Gods but one, for God, alone is the sole creator of all things.

People.

Lord have mercy upon us, and incline our hearts to keep this law.

II. Thou shalt not make to thyself any graven image, nor the likeness of any thing which is in heaven or in earth, in order thereunto to fall down and worship.

Lord have mercy upon us, and incline our hearts to keep this law.

III. Thou shalt not take the name of the Lord thy God in vain, for the Lord will not hold him guiltless that taketh his name in vain.

Lord, have mercy upon us, and incline our hearts to keep this law.

IV. Remember that thou keep holy the sabbath day, six days shalt thou labour, and do what thou hast to do; but the seventh shall be consecrated as a sabbath to the Lord thy God: in it thou shalt not do any manner of work to gain a living, neither shalt thou suffer any of thy family.

Lord, have mercy upon us, and incline our hearts to keep this law.

V. Honor thy father and thy mother, that thy days may be long in the land which the Lord thy God hath given thee.

Lord, have mercy upon us, and incline our hearts to keep this law.

VI. Thou shalt do no murder.

Lord, have mercy upon us, and incline our hearts to keep this law.

VII. Thou shalt not commit adultery.

Lord, have mercy npon us, and incline our hearts to keep this law.

VIII. Thou shalt not steal.

Lord, have mercy upon us, and incline our hearts to keep this law.

IX. Thou shalt not bear false witness against thy neighbour.

Lord, have mercy upon us, and incline our hearts to keep this law.

X. Thou shalt not covet thy neighbour's house, thou shall not covet thy neighbour's wife, nor his man servant, nor his maid servant, nor his ox, nor his ass, nor any thing that is his.

Lord, have mercy upon us, and write all these thy laws in our hearts, we beseech thee.

☞ Here let the minister deliver a sermon, explanatory of one of these commandments, pointing out, with all due simplicity and clearness, the absolute necessity of every person, who wishes to bear the name of a rational creature, exercising his faculties to understand the full meaning of these commandments, and endeavouring to conduct his life in conformity with them. ——— It is the duty of the minister of God, to assist and correct the failings of his cure ; let him therefore, if he perceives any public vice gaining ground among his parishioners, declare from the pulpit his reasons for believing it offensive to God; advise the amendment and correction of it; and let him privately admonish any he may find transgressing the ordinances of God, through passing their lives in an unrighteous manner. —— Let him always addrefs the reafon of his auditors, encouraging them to apply to it at all times; and let him be ready to explain to every one (however low in ftation or weak in abilities) whatever doubts or difficulties may opprefs them; for by this condefcenfion a foul may be faved from perdition; and before the throne of omnipotence, the foul of a poor man is of equal value with that of the moft exalted upon earth.——When the minifter finifhes his difcourfe, let him offer up the following pfalm;

O God, be merciful unto us, and blefs us, and fhew us the light of thy countenance, and be merciful unto us.

That thy way may be known upon earth; thy faving health among all nations.

Let the people praife thee O God: yea, let all the people praife thee!

O let all nations rejoice and be glad; for thou doft judge the folk with righteoufnefs, and doft govern with wifdom every part of thy works.

Let the people praife thee, O God; let all the people praife thee.

O God, blefs us; and let all parts of the world learn to know thee, and to do thy will.

Then shall the earth bring forth her increase; and thou, O God, even our own God, shalt give us thy blessing.

All the Congregation shall say,

Glory be to God, in the highest; and on earth, peace and goodwill towards men.

Prayer.

O God, from whom all holy desires, all good councils and all just works do proceed, give unto thy servants that peace which the world cannot give; that both our hearts may be set to obey thy commandments: and also, that by thee, we being defended, may pass our time in rest and quietness, and in a due performance of the duties taught us by the precepts of Jesus Christ. Amen.

Prayer.

LIGHTEN our darkness, we beseech thee, O Lord; and by thy great mercy, defend us this night from all perils and dangers. Amen.

Let Lessons in the Bible and Testament be here read: Afterwards this Prayer.

O God, the creator and preserver of all mankind, we humbly beseech thee for all sorts and conditions of men; that thou wouldest be pleased to make thy ways known unto them, thy saving health unto all nations. More especially we pray thee for the good estate of thy church; that it may be so guided and governed by thy good spirit, that all who profess and call themselves thy servants, may be led into the way of truth, and may hold the faith in unity of spirit, in the bond of peace, and in righteousness of life. Finally, we commend to thy fatherly goodness, all those who are any ways afflicted in mind, body, or estate: and pray that it may please thee to comfort and relieve them under their several necessities, giving them patience under their sufferings, and a happy issue out of all their afflictions. Amen.

Prayer.

O God, whose nature and property is ever to have mercy and to forgive, receive our humble petitions, and though we be tied and fast bound with the chain of our sins, yet, let the pitifulness of thy great mercy loose us for the honor of thy holy name. Amen.

End of the Evening Service.

N. B. As the parishioners have met together to celebrate the honor of their God, and as music has a great effect in elevating the soul to just ideas, let anthems, properly selected, be now performed; and choral parts, expressive of the greatness of the Almighty, be adapted for the congregation to join in:—And let the evening be passed in a studied attention, to render honor to him who liveth and reigneth for ever, and ever.

COMMUNION.

On the first Sunday in the Month, let the Commemoration of the last Supper of Christ and his Disciples, be celebrated with Piety and thanks—for in the 22d Chapter of St. Luke, we are told of his appointment of it.

" This do in Remembrance of me."

Let therefore a table be covered with a fair Cloth, and let Wine and Bread be set thereon, and the Communicants standing round, let the Minister exhort them as follows.

DEARLY beloved in the Lord, we are met together to celebrate the commemoration of the last supper of Jesus Christ, whose doctrines we acknowledge as the foundation of our hopes; it is therefore our duty to examine ourselves before we presume to eat of that bread, or drink of that cup.

The most perfect being, by every account, that ever was upon earth, after having exerted himself to the utmost in calling mankind to the knowledge of the true God, foresaw that the malice of the jewish priests would prevail, and that his life would be taken away as a sacrifice for having discovered their errors.

Celebrating the passover (which was a high festival with the jews) the friend of mankind perceived the hour was come, when he was to be delivered up to the punishment of death:——Full of virtue, void of pride, he merely forwarned his disciples that his end approached; and after having given thanks, he brake the bread and gave to his disciples, and likewise gave them of the cup, simply commanding,

" This do in remembrance of me."

The benefits which we have received from the communications of Jesus Christ, justly entitle him through the goodness of almighty God, to the high name that is given him by many nations, of Saviour of the world, for before his time idolatry pervaded the whole earth.————It becomes us therefore with thanks and praise, to declare the goodness of the almighty God, and with unfeigned gratitude to acknowledge our sense of the blessings we have received through the life of Christ Jesus; who desired this festival should be kept, that as often as we should meet together to celebrate it, we might consider how boldly he sacrificed his life for the glory of the most high; and that we might be encouraged nobly to sacrifice every present desire, which should in the least interfere with that highest concern, viz. our endeavour to fulfil the will of God;—let us therefore address ourselves to Almighty God, that he will be pleased to send his holy spirit among us to cleanse us from all our sins.

Prayer:

O Omnipotent and all-wife being, thou creator of all things, have favor upon thy humble fervants who offer up their prayers unto thee;—Let thy holy fpirit fanctify us, and impart into us new life;—make us to know, to fear, to love thee :——And grant that the reft of our lives may be conducted to the glory of thee whofe goodnefs, mercy and power are confpicuous in all things.———We thank thee, O God, with our whole hearts, for all thy loving kindnefs to mankind, more efpecially for the knowledge we have received of thee, through Jefus Chrift, whofe life was a proof of his faith and confidence in thee.——— Grant that we who are here met together in all humility to acknowledge thy goodnefs, and to commemorate the laft fupper of Jefus Chrift, may receive the full benefit of thy mercies, through confidering and perceiving the duty of a creature's ftudying to fulfill his maker's will in all things; and therefore, that we may from henceforth exert ourfelves in avoiding the errors and vices of the world.—And, O Lord, as we are fully perfuaded that the conduct of Jefus Chrift was pleafing to thee, fo we befeech thee to grant us thofe powers which will enable us to conduct ourfelves in fuch a manner, that we may anfwer the defign wherefore thou wert pleafed to call us into being. Amen.

All the Congregation.

Pardon our offences, O most high; and strengthen our confidence in thee.

Thou knowest our secret thoughts;—thou knowest the things we ought to ask.

Give unto us, we humbly beseech thee, those things which are necessary to our salvation. Amen. Amen.

Prayer.

O Almighty and ever merciful God, who hadst compassion upon the infirmities of man, and didst impart a true knowledge of thy majesty to the blessed Jesus: We humbly beseech thee, that we, thy creatures, receiving this bread and drinking of this cup in remembrance of that august personage, may be fill'd with gratitude and love towards thee; and thus, continually recalling to our minds the sacrifice which he made, that we may be lead to avoid every offence; in thought, word and deed, to endeavour to glorify thy holy name. Amen.

Minister.

DEARLY beloved, this bread and wine are delivered to you agreeable to the institution of Christ Jesus, that as often as ye meet together to partake of it ye should be induced to examine and consider the intent of the sacrifice he made, when he offered up his life in proof of his confidence in God. Ye know that ye made not yourselves, that all your powers are confined, and that there muſt, of neceſſity, be one ſelfexiſtent being; this being we call God.———Examine every part of creation, his wiſdom and goodneſs are fully diſplayed; and love and fear muſt pervade every reflecting mind.

To this omnipotent Being all honor and praiſe are due;—but we perceive, throughout the world, numbers ignorant of him, and acting contrary to the good of their fellow creatures; hence, we ſee the freedom he has given to man of acting as he thinks covenient to himſelf.

This licence had the effect of producing a general depravity among mankind, but as the laws of God are immutable and all-wiſe, the world could not be prevented from wickedneſs by any extraordinary ſupernatural interpoſition of the Almighty, without deſtroying that free agency, which, perhaps is the grand diſtinction of the race of man in the general ſyſtem of creation, and which, being taken away from man, would be the means of rendering one ſpecies of creatures extinct:—God therefore of his infinite goodneſs, called Jeſus Chriſt to a true knowledge of his attributes, and enabled him to declare to the world thoſe truths which the errors of mankind had obſcured.

By Jeſus Chriſt were the commandments of omnipotence declared, his goodneſs proclaimed, and his power made known to all men.

Let us then, my brethren, when we eat of his bread and drink of this wine, acknowledge with gratitude the goodnefs of God; and let us confider ourfelves as being partakers of the laft fupper of Jefus Chrift;——let us recall to our remembrance, all thofe doctrines which are clearly his;——let us enter into his views, and let us prove ourfelves man the favoured creature of our God; let us feek to know his will,—let us ftudy to fulfill it, and let us draw near and partake of thefe viands in folemn affurance and confirmation to one another, that we believe in one God, as declared by Jefus Chrift; that we thankfully remember the merits of the life of Chrift; and that it is our full determination to endeavour to prove ourfelves worthy the facrifice he made, by fhewing charity to all mankind for the fake of him whom we now celebrate.

One charge more I have to give you,——viz. that this is a folemn act before your God, who knoweth all things and cannot be deceived; fearch therefore your hearts, examine into your fins, fee if any remain which you have not repented of, or whether any malice or wrath is in you that you have not determined to conquer;—if fuch there be, leave, I befeech you, this table, nor think to mock your God; go home, repent of your fins, forgive thofe who have offended you, and come to our next celebration with contrition and fincerity of heart:—And be ye affured that God, upon your fincere repentance, (which he alone can judge of,) and your full determination to avoid offending for the future, will favorably hear thofe prayers you then fhall offer up to him for forgivenefs of the fins with which your confciences have been oppreffed.

The Minifter addreffing himfelf to the Communicants, fhall fay, after breaking the Bread, &c.

TAKE and eat of this bread in remembrance that Chrift gave up his life rather than deny his God.

Take and drink of this cup in remembrance of the blood that Chrift fhed for the fake of mankind,—always recollecting that he died in charity with all men, praying upon the crofs for even thofe who had been his enemies;——and let us, with unfeignednefs, offer unto God the facrifice of thankfgiving in full determination of leading virtuous lives, to the end, that God may be glorified, and may be pleafed to admit us unto a more perfect knowledge of him.

Here let every one offer a gift according to his abilities, and let thefe gifts be applied to the ufe of the poor of the parifh.

The Congregation fhall fay,

We offer up thefe gifts, to thee O God, as an acknowledgment of thy mercies, and in teftimony to one another, that we are in charity with all men.

Then this Pfalm.

Glory be to God on high, and on earth peace and goodwill towards men.

We praife thee, O God; we blefs thee; we worfhip thee; we give thee thanks for thy great glory, O Lord God, our heavenly king; O God, the Father Almighty.

Minister.

THE peace of God which passeth all understanding, keep your hearts and minds in the knowledge and love of God, and in remembrance of the doctrines of Jesus Christ; and the blessings of the one, true, sole, selfexistent, God be among you and remain with you always. Amen.

Form of MATRIMONY.

When the couple to be married and their friends come to the altar, the minister shall address them as follows.

DEARLY beloved, we are here met together in the sight of Almighty God, to hear the plighted troths of these two persons who purpose to pass their lives in unity and love.

The state of matrimony is honorable in every part of the world; altho' many nations differ in their ideas of it. We esteem it the solemn engagement of virtuous persons, made publicly to the community, that they will fulfil the commands of their maker in temperance and chastity; and that they will, to the utmost of their power, perform the duties of good parents:—but marriages are equally sacred without conforming to ceremonies.

Let me beseech ye, who are about to acknowledge each other in the near relation of husband and wife, to consider fully the duties of this state.——— God has given to man the greater strength, and has appointed to woman to bear children, and weakness with necessary confinement is the regular consequence of the birth :— Thus are your duties clearly pointed out to you.

To comfort and protect the woman, to endeavour to ease her from the anxiety she may feel in her time of pain, by mild attentions and tender love; to instruct her and encourage her in all the virtues is the true duty of man.

While the woman, sensible of the weakness of her sex, should exercise that delicate effeminacy which nature has given her, and which is the first delight of man, in submissive yet cheerful love.

Let religious virtue appear in all your actions, and while he affords thee protection, return him thy love with that sweetness which never fails to rivet the affections of man.——And if it shall please the heavenly Father to intrust you with the care of children, let your conduct towards them prove your sense of the duties you owe to God.——— So shall happiness attend you both in this world and in the world to come.

Brethren, attend to the declarations of these persons.

Qu. To the Man.

Is there any other woman whom thou preferrest to this? An.

Qu. To the Woman,

Is there any other man whom thou wouldest wish to marry in preference to this?—An.

Does any one in the congregation doubt their assertions?

Wilt thou N. N. have this woman to thy wife? wilt thou endeavour to fulfil the will of God, in loving her, protecting her, and keeping to her only as long as ye both shall live?—I will.

Wilt thou N. N. have this man to thy husband? and performing the will of God, keep thee only unto him as long as ye both shall live?—I will.

Then shall the Man say
Before this congregation I acknowledge thee N. N. for my wife, and in token whereof, I give thee this ring, engraved with my name; by which, from henceforth, thou shalt be known.

Then shall the Woman say,
Before this congregation I acknowledge thee N. N. for my husband, and in token whereof, I give thee this ring, engraved with my maiden name; which, from henceforth, I will no more use.

Then the Minister shall say,

Brethren, from henceforth respect this couple as man and wife; and may God, of his infinite mercy, bless you.

Prayer.

O God, we beseech thee to bless these thy servants, and to sow the seed of eternal life in their hearts, that whatsoever to thy glory they may undertake they may successfully fulfil :—— And grant, that they, studying thy will in all things, and always being obedient unto it, may be in full safety under thy protection, may abide in thy love unto their lives end, and may finally receive everlasting salvation. Amen.

N. B. The marriage is to be registered—and attested by the minister.

BAPTISM.

DEARLY beloved brethren, for as much as it hath pleased Almighty God that we should be born in ignorance, and that the powers of our reason should, in a great measure, depend upon the cultivation bestowed upon it; it evidently behooves every parent to attend to the education and instruction of his children.——But the salvation of their souls is a concern so great, that our government has thought proper to advife, that there be provided for infants, a new relation, whofe chief concern fhould be to take care that in due time they be inftructed in fuch a knowledge of their own nature, as will lead them to know, and love and fear God:—And to render them worthy of admittance into the kingdom of heaven; by inducing them to pafs their lives as good and virtuous citizens, whereby they will beft prove the fincerity of their profeffions of religion.

Let me therefore exhort you who are to be godfathers and god-mothers of this child, that you will fincerely reflect upon the duties you are about to undertake; not efteeming it a trifling matter of mere form, but fteadfaftly and fincerely purpofing to fulfil the fpirit of the obligation you are now about to lay yourfelves under; confidering, that to you the child is hereafter to think himfelf indebted for the happinefs he may enjoy, or to blame you for the ignorance he may be in and for the mifery he may fuffer, if you wilfully neglect to give him the information neceffary to enable him to conduct himfelf in religious temperance and charity.

To ye therefore, who appear before me as intending to be the parents in God of this child; I now addrefs myfelf:

Will ye, in the name of God, take care that this child fhall be educated in his native language?

Will ye, to the best of your abilities, provide him with useful and good books?

Will ye pay attention to instruct him in the knowledge of God to the best of your abilities?

Will ye call upon him to attend divine service, acquainting him with the duties man is bound to pay to his creator?

Will ye instruct him in the knowledge of his own nature, assisting him with advice whenever he is likely to fall into error?

Will ye call upon him to acquaint himself with those laws of the land in which every individual is concerned?

The God-fathers and God-mothers shall answer,

These we faithfully promise, and we entreat the congregation to join us in prayer to Almighty God, that he will grant a happy result to our endeavours.

Prayer.

ALMIGHTY and everlasting God, we thine humble servants do offer to thee our earnest intreaties, that thou wilt be pleased to call us all to a true knowledge of thee.—— Grant that these sponsors for this child, may ever put that confidence in thy power which will enable them to fulfil the duties they have undertaken.— And, we beseech thee, give thy holy spirit to this infant, that he may early walk in thy way, and may renounce all the covetous desires and vain-glories of this world, which too often take mankind from thy service.

Teach him so to number his days, that, being dead unto sin but alive unto righteousness, he may finally attain to that transcendent blessing, the blessing of a more intimate and spiritual knowledge of thee, his God.———Teach him to know the worth of thy loving mercy when thou wast pleased to furnish Jesus Christ with those lights, whereby he was enabled to dispell the darkness that overshadowed the earth; when mankind served idols, the work of their own hands, instead of serving thee the self-existing God.———To thee, O most Mighty, we address ourselves, in the name and form of prayer of Jesus Christ, beseeching thee to grant us those things which may be beneficial to us.

OUR Father, which art in heaven, hallowed be thy name. Thy kingdom come. Thy will be done on earth, as it is in heaven. Give us this day our daily bread. And forgive us our trespasses as we forgive them that trespass against us. And lead us not into temptation; but deliver us from evil: For thine is the kingdom, and the power, and the glory, for ever and ever, Amen.

DEARLY beloved, this child is now under the care of all its parents; and as from its natural father it will take one name whereby he will be distinguished from other families, so let him now receive another name whereby he may be distinguished as a servant of God.——How shall he be called?——

The Sponsors shall answer.

Minister.

IN the name of the most high God;——be this infant from henceforth called———— — and I sign him with water, and the sign of the cross, in token that ye, his sponsors have undertaken to instruct him in the knowledge of the one God as declared by Jesus Christ, who suffered death upon the cross in proof of his faith in the creator.—— And may the blessing of Almighty God prosper your undertakings. Amen.

BURIAL SERVICE.

Dearly beloved Brethren,

ON————it pleased Almighty God to permit the soul of our brother———— to leave its earthly habitation, whose body we are now about to commit to the grave.

Mortality is annexed to humanity as inevitably as light is to fire; and as it is certain, from natural reason, that our souls or the sensitive part of our frame are distinct from the flesh in which they exist, and may therefore enjoy a separate existence; so we feel a conviction, that in the scheme of providence, there is a state of future rewards for the virtuous, or those who obey the will of their God.

From the uncertainty of the time of our departure from this world, we ought at all times to lead our lives in such a manner, as to be prepared to answer the call of our maker.

Let us therefore, (who now assist at the ceremony of putting this body into the ground.——Ashes to ashes, dust to dust, trusting in the mercy of God, that he will be pleased to call this our departed brother to his rest) take this opportunity of addressing ourselves to the protection of God, that he may bless us in all our endeavours to render ourselves worthy of his love; and that we, being impressed with the idea of the inevitableness of death, may be lead to make this example beneficial to ourselves.

Saint Paul says, " we brought nothing into this world, and it is certain we can take nothing out.—The Lord giveth and the Lord taketh away;——Blessed be the name of the Lord."

The truth of the foregoing is proved every day, and the advantage we ought to make of it, is to reflect on the folly of thofe who, troubling themfelves always about temporal concerns, neglect the confideration of that which is of infinitely greater confequence, viz. The ftate we are to experience hereafter.

No man has returned from the grave to tell us of futurity;—— uncertainty and doubts are the refult of every enquiry: but this we know, that, as there is a good God, he muft have directed every thing proper; and on his mercy we may fafely rely, if we endeavour to fulfil his will while we are on earth.

To us the knowledge of the particulars of the future ftate would be of no ufe, and we may be affured that the uncertainty we labour under is moft advantageous to the general fyftem of creation.————God has confined our duties to this life, and futurity muft difclofe its fecrets to us when we are capable of underftanding them; but this we fhould truft in, that the goodnefs of God will never fail, and that it will be fully extended over every part of the creation.

Yet man that is born of a woman hath but a fhort time to live:——He cometh up and is cut down like a flower; he fleeth as it were a fhadow, and never continueth in one ftay.

In the midft of life we are in death; of whom may we feek for fuccour but of the Lord?

O God, most holy; O Lord most mighty; O Holy and blessed creator, deliver us from the bonds of sin.

Then shall we cry with exultation. O Death! where is thy Sting? O Grave! where is thy Victory?

Thanks be to God, who forgiving us our sins, hath given us the victory.

Prayer.

O Almighty and everlasting God, who hatest nothing that thou hast made, nor desirest the death of a sinner, but rather that he should turn from his wickedness and live: Look down with favor on thy humble servants, who acknowledge their transgressions, and who beseech thee to grant them forgiveness of their sins. They confess, with contrition, that their thoughts are too often drawn away, by the cares of the world, from the due consideration of a future state; and that their actions are too frequently unworthy of beings who are in expectation of immortality.————But to thee, who art the God of all goodness, we address ourselves, and pray, that thou wouldest be pleased to impress our minds with such a sense of the necessity of attending to our duties, that we may accomplish whatsoever thou expectest from creatures whom thou hast favored with faculties, whereby they may know their God; yet to whom thou haft given free agency—— We fee, by the end of this our brother, whofe body we have juft committed to the earth, as well as by the experience of every day, that death is the inevitable lot of all men; and that thou, at an unknown time, doft require that we fhould refign our fouls and fhould no more live on earth ————But, O Creator, we have heard with our ears, and our fathers have declared unto us, the noble works which thou didft in their days and in the old time before them.———We believe, that thefe thy noble works would not have been performed, hadft not thou defigned for man, a future ftate of fenfe, when, having left his prefent habitation, he fhall more diftinctly know that God, whofe power and goodnefs he had feen on earth.——We have been taught by Jefus Chrift, that thy favor will be fhewn to thofe alone who do thy will, whilft vindictive judgments fhall be iffued againft fuch as are finners and difobedient to the dictates of their reafon.——We know, O Lord, the frailties of our nature, and how many are the tranfgreffions of mankind: But we alfo believe that thy mercies are unbounded, that thy judgments are ever lenient, and that thy forgivenefs is ever accorded to the truely repentant finner.———— Give unto us, O omnipotent and all perfect Being, fuch a knowledge of thee as may lead us to a fincere repentance of thofe fins which we have heretofore committed, and may induce us in

K

the time to come, to study to know and perform our duties to thee, and our relative duties to all our fellow creatures.————Give us hearts, to love, assist, and comfort one another in the full perfection of that system of universal charity which the blessed Jesus taught to his disciples.————Teach us to be grateful to thee for his life, his sufferings, his death; and grant, that whenever we assist at the ceremony of interring a fellow creature, we may recall to our minds the resignation of Jesus, which could alone proceed from the sense of having in all things faithfully fulfilled thy will; and give unto us, that at our deaths we may receive alike comfort from a similar confidence in thee. Grant, O Father, that we worthily thinking of Christ's death, may be more strongly urged to do those acts which thy wonderful scheme of creation makes it the duty of every being to perform: and grant that, whenever it shall please thee to call us from this state of existence, our deaths may be no ways terrible to us, through having our bosoms comforted with these reflections; that although we are offenders yet that our judge is merciful, and that he is evermore ready to forgive than to punish. To thee, O God, whose perfections are unspeakable; whose goodness is unbounded; whose selfexistent nature is incomprehensible to man; we offer up our praise; blessed be thy name O God for ever and ever! Amen.

CHURCHING OF WOMEN.

Minister.

FOR as much as it hath pleased Almighty God to give you safe deliverance, and to preserve you in child-birth; you shall therefore give hearty thanks unto God, and say,

I am well-pleased that the Lord hath heard the voice of my prayer, therefore will I call upon him as long as I live:

For my soul was full of trouble; and my flesh was oppressed with pain:

And I cried to the Lord God of my salvation, and he permitted my prayer to enter into his presence:

And his mercy delivered me; and my travail was at an end.

What return can I make unto the Lord for his goodness, or for all the benefits he has done unto me?

I will pay my vows now, in the presence of his people; I will declare his truth, and will speak of his mercies, which reach above the clouds.

Teach me thy way, O Lord, and I will walk in thy truth: O knit my heart unto thee, that I may fear thy name.

I thank thee, O God, with my whole heart; I will praife thy name for ever and ever.

For great was thy mercy toward me;—I was in mifery and thou helpedft me.

To be omitted if the Child is dead. {

And thou reftoredft me to my family with honor and with fame:

For thou permittedft me to bring forth a child, who hereafter may be admitted to the knowledge of his God.

Teach him thy ftatutes, O God, and render thy paths delightful unto him.

So fhall he be lead to ferve thee, in humblenefs and lownefs of heart, and to walk in thy ways all the days of his life.

Happy is the man who is thus bleffed in his children; happy is the family who faithfully ferve the Lord!

Turn again unto thy reft, O my foul, for the Lord hath rewarded thee.

For he hath faved thee from death and the condemnation of finners.

Join with me in praises all ye his people? O let us always praise the Lord?———Blessed be thy holy name O God, for ever and ever. Amen.

Minister.

O Almighty God, we give thee humble thanks for that thou hast vouchsafed to deliver this woman, thy servant, from the great pain of child-birth;——— Grant, we beseech thee most merciful father, that she, through thy help, may both faithfully live and walk according to thy will in this life present; and may also be partaker of everlasting glory in the world to come, through performing thy will, and through faith in thy mercies as declared by Jesus Christ, in whose name and words we further call upon thee.

OUR Father, which art in heaven, hallowed be thy name. Thy kingdom come. Thy will be done on earth as it is in heaven. Give us this day our daily bread; and forgive us our trespasses as we forgive them that trespass against us. And lead us not into temptation but deliver us from evil: For thine is the kingdom, and the power, and the glory for ever and ever. Amen.

E N D.

CERTAIN REGULATIONS DICTATED
By *JACOBUS VERITAS.*

Not enforced by Acts of Parliament but left to the option of the Parishes.

BETWEEN morning and evening services I would have the chief people of the parish meet together and consult upon the best means of relieving any of the parishioners, who through poverty or illness, are afflicted with distress:——I would likewise have them enquire into the morals of every one, and where errors appear, take proper steps to correct them.——If any are idle or vicious, let them be exhorted to a contrary behaviour, and if exhortation fails, let them be sent into confinement, that they may have leisure to perceive wherein they have been wrong.

I would likewise wish all my subjects both rich and poor, to be provided with one similar plain dress, which they should wear when they went into the church on a sunday:———Not that any particular religious act is hereby intended by the ceremony of dress, but merely to encourage cleanliness among all the parishioners, and to enable every one to make a proper appearance when before the throne of God.——But the effect will not rest here, for it will assist the minister in inspiring the congregation with a just sense of the real confequence of man; by humbling the proud and exalting the lowly and meek.————This 'drefs I would wifh to be provided by the parifh at a general expence, and no difcriminating alteration to be admitted from the higheft to the loweft.

Let every individual be entrufted with the care of his own drefs, but let him be required to be careful of it, under pain of cenfure of the meeting, who fhall deprive him of it for any offence, which they think requires this punifhment, until his contrition fhall have worked out his pardon.

Likewife at this meeting, let the leffons for the next funday be felected, taking care to chufe fuch as may afford the minifter an opportunity of affifting the underftandings of the weak, by bringing them to a due fenfe and knowledge of the Lord and his will.—And let them be felected in the due courfe, till the whole bible and teftament are gone through.——— Once in every three months let fome part of the Alcoran of Mahomet be read, and let the minifter make fuch commentaries thereon as he thinks proper.

And in cafe upon any particular occafion it fhould appear neceffary that other prayers fhould be added to thofe already appointed, let the minifters prepare them, and fubmit them to the church-wardens and heads of the parifh, for their approbation and correction. *

---

* Thefe regulations are every where ftrictly attended to, and the people fulfil with eagernefs, all the wifhes of their founder.

Having thus given you their form of prayer, I fhall, in order to elucidate their religious opinions, introduce fome difcourfes that are publifhed in Veritas-———The three firft are fuppofed to have been prepared and delivered by Jacobus Veritas, himfelf.--And are now generally read in all their churches, on the firft three fundays in the year—the laft difcourfe is a later produ&tion.

RELIGIOUS DISCOURSES,

As delivered by the Veritafian Clergy.

Difcourfe the Firft.

DEARLY beloved, in that part of the book of pfalms which we this morning read, we found the following fentence,

Lord! what is man that thou art mindful of him? or the fon of man that thou fo regardeft him?

This text, in all the countries through which I have travelled, is a favourite of preachers of every denomination, and they ufe it to enable them to difplay the wonderful goodnefs of God, in preferving the children of men.

To make it a wonder that God fhould be mindful of creatures whom he hath called into exiftence, is a proof of wanting that knowledge which would teach us to fee every thing, as the wife contrivance of a beneficent creator.

Thefe words were ufed by the pfalmift, to exprefs his fenfe of the inferiority of man, when his mind had been employed in contemplating the power of God.

The wonderful superiority of the selfexistent being must inevitably fill, with the most reverential awe, whatever human breast contemplates his perfections:—But to suppose that his providence is at any time regardless of his works, is judging of his nature, as if he were equally liable to change his plans, as human beings, whose shortsightedness and limitted powers prevent them from knowing every circumstance which may be annexed to any future event, and therefore they cannot avoid altering and amending their opinions, according as new objects present themselves unto them.

But with God it is otherwise, his prescience prevents him from the possibility of change; and his omniscience enables him to discover every result, even before the means are prepared to produce it.

The power of God is displayed through all his works, and his goodness is ever acting for their support; for it would argue a want of power, consequently of perfection, were it possible for the supreme being, for one moment, to leave creation unregulated.

We will quit the idea which is annexed to the words of the text, expressive of the kindness of God, in regarding the children of men; and will take this opportunity of enquiring into that most useful question, what is man?

To this, it may be anfwered generally,—that man is a created being, capable of obferving events; of combining and feparating ideas; of judging from paft circumftances of the *probability* of the future; and poffeffing faculties whereby he can communicate his fentiments to others :———— His nature animal, partaking of its general properties, and his grand diftinction from other annimals is his mental powers.

Upon examining into this defcription, we find ourfelves to be of this order in creation; if we look around us we perceive man evidently occupying the firft rank in the world, and making fubfervient and of ufe to himfelf every other creature.

Enquiring further into our nature, we find it a compounded one;——we feel wants; we are fubject to infirmities; we are liable to many accidents in common with other animals; but at the fame time, we perceive that our powers are vaftly fuperior to theirs, and that the moft ignorant of the human race is capable of afferting this difference, even over the moft formidable of the brute creation.

In the ftate of fociety, we find the faculty whereby we acquire this fuperiority, and which we call reafon, capable of the moft wonderful extention and improvement.

By the assistance of reason we provide for every necessary of life with all the caution of prescient beings, and the mutations that are discoverable in nature are turned to our advantages.

This faculty, we have it in our power to enlarge, and we perceive that it is distinct from the body:— for sometimes when the body is at rest, and animal nature incapable of motion, the mind is actively employed; while on the contrary, sometimes our animal nature seems to act as a mere mechanical work ungoverned or unaffected by reason.

Hence, we conclude, that man is compounded of a spiritual as well as corporeal substance; and his spiritual part has been called by the name of soul.

The soul of man, or his spiritual part, requires our utmost consideration, in as much as it is not perceptable to any of our corporal faculties, but is discoverable only from the exertions of those powers themselves which constitute what we may call the soul; and in no persons is the conviction of our possessing a soul distinct from the body, yet connected with it so strong as in those who have most attentively examined into it.

When I first asked myself,—what is man? confusion filled my mind, and I could make no other reply than, that I was a created being; because, I found it impossible for me to make myself.——— Immediately this question followed,—who created me?

I cast my eyes around the world, I no where saw a being of greater powers than man; I knew his incapacity to create, and I answered, " I am the creature of " an invisible being."

Who then created this invisible being?——— I soon discovered the necessity of one, selfexistent, Being, as a first cause of all things, and I was convinced of the impossibility of a created being, forming just ideas of self-existence.

This selfexistent being is our God.

We examine into his essence and are filled with wonder at his perfections; and we join with the psalmist in expressing our sense of his greatness.

After thus acknowledging a creator, the soul enquires into its own nature, and at length perceives that its state of existence in the human body is but for a certain time, that the body dies, and that its own fate is involved in uncertainty; because, although every day furnishes us with proofs of the inevitability of this end of man, yet does not any soul return from the grave, to acquaint us with the circumstances that happen after death.

The consideration of the great powers of the soul, whereby we seem to enjoy a different being from the rest of the creatures upon earth, has in most ages induced men to believe in a future state; and they have received as a convincing proof of the certainty of it, that the creator would not have permitted the pains which some men feel in this world, nor the unequal distribution of its comforts, unless he had provided a place of future happiness, where they might meet with a recompense for every thing they had suffered:—and then, noticing the wickedness of many, they have concluded, that a place of punishment would certainly be prepared for such sinners.

This doctrine of the immortality of the soul, and a state of future rewards and punishmeuts has been taught by most of the learned, among the ancients; and their poets have left us descriptions of the palaces, and groves, and delights, which filled their elysium or place of rewards; and also, of the torments that are practised upon those who were condemned to suffer them.

Various Gods are described, and various employments alloted them; but the ancients, although totally void of the religious ideas we possess, concurred in this, that man is a dependant creature, and that his soul will be sensible after death.

In these later days, it has pleased the Almighty Creator to permit a light to shine upon the world, to dispel the clouds and darkness in which our fore-fathers were lost.

Bigotry and superstition have vanished before us; we know ourselves and our God; and we have no doubt of a futurity; but still we see how liable humanity is to err, by observing the different opinions of the different nations of the world, in their present ideas of God.

Fortunately for us, my brethren, we are in a country where all prejudices are banished; where the first doctrines which we are taught are, that we are created beings whom the creator has furnished with reason, in order to enable us, by applying to it, to judge of what is proper for us. ——And, we likewise have the necessity of thus applying to, and judging from our own reasons alone, pointed out to us in a clear and rational manner. No mysterious concealments; no dark interpretations of things which the human mind is incapable of conceiving are here given; nor is the declaration of a belief which a man cannot understand, made an article of salvation. Nor do we require any of those absurdities, which our books inform us other nations esteem of the greatest consequence.——Our doctrines are perfectly simple, and adapted to every capacity.——We say, that there is one God; that he is good and all perfect;——that he made every thing capable of performing what he required from it;—— and that the man who acts strictly in conformity with the dictates of his reason, cannot be displeasing to his God.

An all-perfect and good felfexiftent being could only begin creation from the defire of difpenfing happinefs, and after having provided his creatures with every thing neceffary thereto, would only lay this command, do not abufe my bounty.

Man then was created fit for the enjoyment of the things which were provided for his happinefs; and was furnifhed with faculties that would enable him, if properly exercifed, to conquer thofe propenfities of his animal nature, which would otherwife tend to defeat the end of his being.

The powers of his mind affift him in foaring above this world, and he commands and controuls all the inferior parts of creation with a decided fuperiority.

It is evident, that God has appointed man to be a free agent, and has left all his actions uncontrouled by any higher power:—— From hence, likewife it is reafonable to fuppofe, that thofe who conduct their lives according to what they muft know is the will of the creator, will be hereafter rewarded; but that thofe who act otherwife will meet with their deferts.

Reafon is a gift from God, but neverthelefs dependant, in fome meafure, upon ourfelves, . in as much as due cultivation is neceffary to bring forth its powers.

By reason alone, is man able to know his God, and the first duty incumbent upon man, must necessarily be this, to exercise the faculties which he possesses, to the utmost of his power, in order to attain a due knowledge of the creator: — And this seems to be required of us, because the deity does not make himself known to our senses in any way, except in his works, all of which bespeak the highest wisdom and power.

When I have resided in foreign countries, I have been much offended at hearing all arguments on religious subjects avoided, by the people declaring, that it was not fit for them to enter upon such subjects, because they were unequal to the task.

Would they themselves be satisfied with a similar answer from any one of their servants, whom they had furnished with every thing requisite to fulfil his duty; when censuring him for having neglected it would they be satisfied with being told?

' That indeed it was true, he had been provided with
' what might, perhaps, be necessary, but he could not
' tell that, and therefore he did not try."——They would not;——and yet, they suppose that the Almighty will not demand of them, why they have not used the talent he has given them:———but this, I am afraid, is to be attributed to priestcraft.

M

The clergy in other countries enter into the profeſſion for bread, and if you read their hiſtories, you will find as much traffic in this as in any other article of trade.————Their intereſt it is to keep up their credit, which can be done only by fettering the minds of the laity.

There are many of them who ſpeak of the attributes of the deity with all propriety imaginable, but at the ſame time, they join therewith ſuch abſurdities as tend to deſtroy thoſe attributes.

The truſting to reaſon, is repreſented as highly improper in their auditors who, they ſay, ſhould be ſenſible that they cannot know ſo much as their paſtors, whoſe ſtudies have been entirely devoted to religious enquiries. They diſplay their own learning with all the powers of language, and endeavour to gain full poſſeſſion of the minds of their pariſhioners.———— They tell them, this book we read (being the ſame as our bible and teſtament) is a revelation from God; that they muſt believe every thing contained in it.————That it is a damnable offence to doubt it ; and that is preſumption to enquire into the truth of its being a revelation from God.———— Thus eſtabliſhing the ſacredneſs of this book, they ſelect parts of it, which they explain according to their intereſt, and are particularly fond of the text,

" The heart of man is deceitful above all things."

from whence they shew the impropriety of a man trusting it in judging for himself, and they prepare their auditors for whatever they think proper to deliver.

Hence absurd unintelligible doctrines are taught; and mysteries are propounded; when they find themselves in a dilemma they produce what they call their authority, which they declare to be the word of God, and therefore true.

That the word of God must be true is most certain, but whether what they call the word of God is so or not, remains to be proved.

Let us briefly examine this; it must be admitted, that whatever it pleaseth God to declare unto men, must be of the utmost consequence;———that his declaration must be perfectly adapted to their capacities; and that nothing unnecessary, nothing superfluous would be revealed by God:—Will the books in question stand these tests?— *they will not!*

Let us have done with this, and examine further, what is reason?

This power of the human mind, which is distinguished in its nature from the instinct of animals, borders upon it so much that it is difficult to draw the line where instinct ends and reason begins; yet, we know, that the brute creation do not give any signs of several ideas, which, perhaps every human being possesses.—reason may be best defined, the power of comparing and drawing consequences from ideas that have no immediate connection with the animal œconomy,

By reason, we are able to reflect upon our own nature, and from thence, to form ideas of that Being, whose essence neverthelefs escapes our most arduous search;———but the enquiring into his attributes necessarily leads us to discover his probable intention in creating us; and we readily assent to the position,—that we are bound to fulfil his will in all things.

We quickly perceive that the human nature possesses a perfection superior to the rest of animated creation; and gratitude at least is a return we are bound to make, to God for the favors received; but we cannot do this properly without knowing our real situation in this world.

The consequence of man has been greatly magnified by many writers, while others have represented him as a being whose follies debase him beneath the rest of animated nature.

The first have gone so far as to say, the Almighty Eternal God looked upon mankind of so much value, as to have been induced to lay down his own life, to redeem them from their sins.

The latter have raked together all the wickedness that was ever committed upon the earth; and in describing man, have painted a true picture of the being of whom we have read under the name of beelzebub.

Were the orb upon which we live, the only one which moved in the regions of space.————Were all the power of the supreme exhausted in this work, we then might give some credit to the doctrines of the former.

Or were we satisfied, that, having made the world, God had placed upon it a set of beings on purpose to torment each other, we might then credit the latter; but upon enquiry into both these opinions, we shall find them partial and contrary to the fact; the one being ignorant of the great Creator; the other excluding all good from the world.

Upon using our reason, we obtain indubitable proofs of numberless other worlds; the work of the same supreme power who made us and our world; and every star that we see, may be the habitation of millions of sensible creatures.

What proof can be given us, that God would die to redeem all thofe worlds? and why fhould we fuppofe he died to redeem this one?——In faɛt, the doɛtrine is abfurd.————God cannot die :————He cannot ceafe to exift :———Nor if it was in his power, would all creation be of fufficient confequence to occafion it.————Nor, indeed, could good arife therefrom; for the moment that the period fhould arrive, when God no more exifted, creation would no longer be upheld, and Chaos would return again.—————The people that he laid down his life to fave, would be deftroyed for want of his proteɛting providence; and the reft of the innocent worlds would perifh, through his cruel kindnefs for a fmall number of animated beings who had grofsly offended him.

Some men, thinking too highly of themfelves, have credited the doɛtrine that God did die for man; and have yielded up their reafon to gratify the pride of their hearts.

Many nations to this day believe, or fay they believe, the fame; even the people among whom I was born, though they have cleanfed their religion from many fuperftitions, yet have fuffered this doɛtrine to remain; but if you look into the lives of thefe people you will find them, in general, paffed contrary to thofe direɛtions which they profefs to believe were left them by their God.

Almost every kind of vice is practised among them; they injure themselves; they injure one another; and break through what they declare to be the express commands of their God, with all the ingratitude of that creature which they denominate the devil.—Yet they have the folly to say, that faith in the promises of Christ will wash away all their sins.

By them, reason and faith are generally set in opposition to one another, which most assuredly is very improper; for faith, as one of their authors, justly, observes, is nothing but a firm conviction, and consequent assent of the mind, which cannot be given to any thing but upon good reason.

If a man says he believes, and yet does not comprehend his assertion, he lies against his own soul, and his hypocrisy will not be unrewarded;—and he that believes without having any reason for his belief, is at best but merely in love with his own fancies; but surely he does not do justice to himself, nor does he pay a proper obedience to his maker, who would have him use those discerning faculties he has given him to keep him out of errors.

True religion proceeds from a just sense of the creator; not that it is possible for man to form perfect ideas of this selfexistent being, for God is incomprehensible to our prefent nature, and all that we know of him is negative.

We are not able to declare what he is, but we know what he is not; and therefore our minds being fatisfied that he cannot be imperfect, firmly declare his attributes of perfection.

Being free from unworthy ideas of the moft higheft, we, my friends, affure ourfelves that the creator is beft pleafed, when the univerfal harmony he planned is undeftroyed by thofe beings, whofe happinefs depends upon the uninterrupted exchange of benefits which he intended fhould take place throughout all creation; and we believe that God made all things fufficiently perfect to accomplifh the purpofes expected from them.

Let me therefore entreat you all to exercife your reafon; ftudy to improve it; apply to it in all things, and pray to your creator, that he will affift you in all your difficulties: Seek to know him;—acquaint yourfelves with his attributes;—and walk humbly before him, in virtue, all the days of your lives.

DISCOURSE THE SECOND.

WE will devote this morning to the contemplation of the attributes of the Almighty and invisible Creator; and to the consideration of the principal different religions of mankind.

The mind, when first impelled to endeavour to acquaint itself with the divine essence, is astonished at the incomprehensibility of it, and almost giving up the attempt, acknowledges at once, the greatness, wisdom, and power of the selfexistent:———And like the eye, which has incautiously looked against the sun, is overpowered with the refulgent splendor that breaks upon it.

Let not presumption ever enter into our hearts; but as rational beings, let us, with humility, reverence, and fearful love, so use the faculties which the omnipotent hath given us, that when an account shall be required from us, we may prove ourselves to have been not unprofitable stewards.

If man has any superiority over the rest of the world, it is in those gifts whereby he is rendered capable of knowing the goodness of his God; and in the due cultivation of those blessings ought man to employ the greatest part of his time:———Nor need he fear exercising his powers to too great an extent, for those things which are improper for man to know can never be discovered by him.

The attribute of God, which naturally presents itself to our view whenever we turn our thoughts towards the consideration of his being is Selfexistence; but of this we can form no clear ideas.

All our knowledge arises from experience, and that combination of ideas, which proceeds from the recollection of those objects which have affected our senses.—We perceive every object of our senses to be an effect; not one being indued with the power of self-creation;—and therefore we are convinced that there is a first selfexistent cause who is invisible.—Thus far our reason abstractedly discovers, but our souls are seldom content; and we examine further into the nature of this first cause.

Selfexistence, we are soon satisfied only belongs to one; yet has the argument been sometimes maintained in the schools, that there is more than one selfexistent being; but this seems mere logical subtlety, which no body can prove or refute, owing to our total ignorance of the nature of selfexistence; and, if we apply to our reason, we shall receive this solution,—if there be two selfexistent beings, they must be independent; and they must have separate governments; we being an effect, must proceed from one first cause, who, with respect to us, is solely selfexistent:—There is then but one selfexistent being.

Nothing on earth is free from certain regulations: nothing is independent of particular ones: we see the whole is ordered in the best manner possible, which clearly denotes infinite wisdom and power in the great first cause.

Birth and weakness are every where conjoined; every thing at first is in a state of growth; and different periods are assigned to different creatures, ere they attain their greatest perfection; at this time there seems to be a small stop, but soon decay commences, quickly after the creature looses its powers, its component parts gradually perish and seem to vanish from our sight.

That this regular course may be kept up, all creatures are permitted to continue their species when they arrive at certain periods of perfection; and the care of its off-spring is rendered absolutely necessary to the happiness of every part of the animal creation.

To these regulations man is also subject :—He is born, he dies, his flesh rots, his bones decay, and dust is all that remains of his so glorious being.———— So soon as his pulse has ceased to beat, and his breath has departed from him, his body becomes a wretched corpse, and no experiments of tortures can make him shew the least appearance of sense.

The brute creation and mankind are here on an equality, their ends bearing the strongest similitude; some die in pain, others finish their lives without a struggle; but none escape this inevitable doom of death.

If we examine into the internal structure of men and animals, and call to our assistance the experience of the anatomist, we shall find the same regular conformity; bones to support the muscles; muscles and sinews appointed to give actions to the bones; and a brain to direct the action.

Even in this seat of sense, the brain, do the same appearances present themselves unto us; nor can we point out an anatomical difference, to assign a reason why other animals are not furnished with equal powers to man.

Our wants are the same; and if I may be allowed the expression, a similar dissimilarity is discoverable in our tempers.———— Whence then arises the difference?

Solely, may we answer, from the permission of God!

It will be perceived by the attentive enquirer, that the earth is filled with a regular chain of creatures;

and that the three grand fyſtems, animal, vegetable, and mineral are wonderfully linked together, although their moſt perfect parts ſeem totally diſtinct.

Man, who is clearly the head of every being that lives upon this earth, ſeems poſſeſſed of one grand diſtinction, which ſeparates him from all the reſt;—that is, the uſe of ſpeech in its full extent, nor can any other diſtinction be found ſufficiently declaratory of his ſpecies. For the link which joins him to the brute creation, has been known to give proofs of having reflecting powers, more extended than are found in many men.

Moſt creatures utter ſounds, but they are only expreſſive of their preſent paſſions, while man reflecting on thoſe paſt events which did not any ways affect him, declares his thoughts of future occurrences with clearneſs and preciſion:—In ſhort, he proves his title to the faculty we call reaſon, is thereby alone diſtinguiſhed from other created animals, and is thereby enabled to know his God.

By the due cultivation of his reaſon, man makes himſelf worthy of the ſtation which he is called to fill in the univerſe; and by neglect of it he debaſes himſelf to a level with the brutes, who do not ſeem to be acquainted with a deity.

As there cannot be a doubt in the mind of any thinking person, of the selfexistence of God, although inexplicable by us, let us next consider his other attributes.

The attribute of omnipotence is given him from all our faculties evincing his title to it.———For can the eye which has beheld the face of the earth and has seen the stars, with all the glory of the heavens? Can the mind which has been used to reflect on all space being filled with creation, and has looked upon the sun, as it really is, the immense fountain of heat and light to a system of worlds, revolving round it in regular stated periods; to which system our earth belongs?——Can this mind refrain from exclaiming? how great is thy power O God! Truly thou art omnipotent! It surely cannot; and in this point of view the omnipotence of God strikes us in the most forcible manner.

The wisdom of God is sufficiently proved, by the harmony that is perceptible throughout all nature; every thing being at once assisting and assisted;——not one necessary or want can be discovered unprovided for, and use and comfort are every where conjoined.

God's attribute of omnipresence or being every where, arises from the conviction we feel within us, that if the providence of the deity were at any period absent from his works, they muſt inevitably fall to ruin :——. Beſides, from this, proceeds his attribute of omniſcience, or knowledge of all things, and theſe are ſo intimately connected, that if we could deny the one we muſt object to the other, which would argue a manifeſt imperfection in that being who is all-perfect.

Immortality, or eternal duration is another attribute of God, and is equally as inconceivable to man as ſelf-exiſtence; but nevertheleſs, the mind agrees to it, becauſe it feels its own limited powers, and becauſe it is ſatisfied that the ſelfexiſtent can never die.

Of the goodneſs of God, the world itſelf furniſhes us with proofs, which ſpeak to our reaſon and addreſs us through our ſenſes. How admirably adapted to the comforts of his creatures, has he provided every thing which is neceſſary for their well being! The food we take, not only recruits our ſtrength, but affords us pleaſing ſenſation while we eat it; and our ſleep is the effect of the bleſſing of a good creator, who wills the happineſs of his creatures.———All our ſenſes are the inlets of delights, and we are formed for joy and for gratitude.———Yet it has been aſked by many people of other nations, why is there unhappineſs in the world?———How does it agree with the goodneſs of God to ſuffer pain and diſeaſe?

To such questions I have answered——ye have not known God?

Unhappiness is far from being a destined lot of humanity.——Pain and disease are generally attendants upon our offences against our nature, and are not to be mentioned as an imputation upon the goodness of the omnipotent.

This orb, it is true, is filled with mortals, whose infirmities make them complain, and our nature is indeed liable to accidents, no human being can avoid. But to the errors, the ignorance, and vices of mankind, are to be ascribed the chief of the evils of which man complains.——Man does not take the proper steps to avoid them; in fact he seems to seek them, and then, too often, impiously charges the supreme with want of goodness.

From whence do the horrors of war, which lay whole countries in ruin, proceed? but from man's injustice and ambition.

From whence come the chief diseases of his body? but from his intemperance and imprudence.——This nation bears witness to the goodness of God; but its virtues are conspicuous among all nations.

Which of our children would suffer unavailing lamentations, or impious ejaculations to pass their lips, because they accidentally felt pain?. not one!

they may figh from the exquifitenefs of torture, but their minds will never harbour a thought againft the goodnefs of our God.———— Confcious of favors before received, and which they make no doubt will in future be repeated; their prefent painful interval, they hope, will not be long, and they find comfort in the thought, that their God is not difpleafed with their refignation.

From ignorance alone can the doubts of the goodnefs of God have proceeded,——and from this caufe, have arifen the errors of mankind:——How careful then ought we to be to cultivate our reafon!——How fufpicious of thofe doctrines which teach us to fear to ufe it!

How good does the character of that man feem, who expends all his fuperfluous wealth in affifting the poor and needy!——We admire the man and we approve his conduct!——But how far doth the goodnefs of God, as difplayed through all the world, exceed every thing of which human nature is capable!——Amply has he furnifhed this world with whatever is defirable by man, and he has permitted him the free ufe of every thing, with merely the prohibition, that he fhould abufe nothing.

Gratitude is due from man to God for even the pains he fuffers, as thereby he is checked in many things, which he would otherwife heedlefsly purfue to his ruin; And this will appear clear to the reflecting mind, *that if any* alteration fhould be made in our *nature*, the animal *man would be loft* to creation.

For, throughout the whole fyftem with which we are acquainted we cannot find any part of fpace either unufeful or wanting of inhabitants.—Progreffive perfection is clearly feen, and man ftands confeffed the fuperior animal, whofe exiftence is appointed to be on the earth.

The human mind, unconfined within its earthly dwellings, foars above the limits of this world, and fees innumerable orbs fufpended as it were in the heavens;—judging from every thing on earth, it does not hefitate to believe that the God, who has fo artfully and amply filled this globe with every thing adapted to it, has not left thofe fplendid orbs unoccupied by creatures who may know their God:——Thus our reafon readily concludes, that there are other beings in other worlds, poffeffing equal or fuperior powers to thofe of man; and that, if man were rendered more perfect than he at prefent is, he would become a different fpecies of creature, and would partake of a nature adapted to another fituation. Even in this, therefore, is the goodnefs of God ftill vifible.

In all probability, there are a continued chain of beings rifing in a regular progreffion towards perfection, till the links ſtop at the unpaſſable bound, which muſt ever be between created nature and the incommunicable attributes of the deity, *viz.* ſelfexiſtence, omnipotence and full perfection.

Often have I explored the regions of immeaſurable ſpace in order to find the particular habitation of my God: I have examined the planets that revolve around the ſun, and the ſtars that are fixed in the remoteſt diſtances.—— I have fancied to myſelf ſtill other worlds, harmoniouſly ſituate at like enormous diſtances, even beyond the fixed ſtars; but yet, no place could I conceive worthy the favor of the creator's particular preſence. Loſt and bevildered in the idea, I have ſhrunk from the contemplation, and retiring within myſelf, my reaſon has informed me that the ſearch was vain; for that the eſſence of the deity is inconceivable to human nature, our ſenſes not being adapted to this knowledge: But the attempt was not totally void of benefit; I found my mind capable of ſoaring into other worlds above the earth.—— I had paſſed in idea, from one to another; I perceived life and ſenſe throughout the whole; and I ſaw the proofs of the greatneſs of my God.——Incapable of long ſupporting theſe thoughts, my mind has turned to the conſideration of its own nature, and of the ways of my fellow creatures:—I have obſerved every nation differing in their opinions of God, while all were guilty of errors that tended to defeat what has appeared to me his deſign in creation.

The duty of employing my abilities, in order to avoid error, appeared in the ſtrongeſt point of view; and I determined to examine freely into the opinions of every nation, and afterwards to draw my own concluſions.

The people among whom I was born call themſelves chriſtians and declare their belief, that God came down upon earth in the form of a man, took upon himſelf our nature, and ſuffered the people he was among to deſtroy him as an impoſtor.

Other nations deny that it was God who came upon earth, but only a prophet, who was ſent to prepare the way for a greaṭer prophet, who was to ſcourge mankind for their ſins:—and who, when he came, propagated his religion with fire and the ſword, and declared that there is but one God, that himſelf was his prophet, to whom God frequently revealed his will, which he as conſtantly publiſhed to the people.

One ſect I find diſperſed through all the world, without king, government, or poſſeſſion of territory; hated by the reſt of mankind, yet calling themſelves the favoured nation of God;——their writings declaring, that, in former times, God had perſonal communication with ſome of their nation, and that he inſpired their prophets with the knowledge of future events.——This nation, even according to their own accounts, were impious and wicked, continually forgetting their God, who had mercifully declared unto them his laws, which they perpetually tranfgreffed.———Wearied with their fins, God, at at length, is faid to have pronounced a curfe upon them, and to have difperfed them, a race of vagabonds over the face of the earth, unverfally defpifed and detefled by the reft of mankind;—— until after a period of years expiration fhall be paffed, when they expect to be reftored to their ancient kingdom.

Other nations there are who worfhip images, the works of their own hands, and pray to them in all their diftreffes.

To me it affords a caufe for grief, when I confider humanity in this inferior flate, and I figh with compaffion at the thought; but at the fame time my gratitude is raifed towards my God, who called me into being, in a nation, and at a time, when religious enquiry was unfettered by the reftraints of bigotry and fuperftition.

To paint to onefelf the poor idolator, cutting from the foreft a tree that pleafeth him,—lopping its boughs, warming himfelf by the fire he has made with them, and worfhipping the trunk from which he has taken them,—is a picture that is far from affording plea-ture. — Nor indeed could we suppose it possible for human nature to be so blind, but that we know it for a fact, that at this present time, whole nations are in this state of blindness.

The absurdity of this worship is self-evident, and I turn again my attention to the Jewish religion.

The Jews say that the bible was written by the particular inspiration of God, and they call it the book of their law.——They inform us, according to this book, that there was a man named Moses, to whom God communicated what had passed from the beginning of the world, and whom he commanded to write the account for the benefit of his nation.

In the first chapter of Genisis, we are informed of the nature of the creation of the world; which according to that account, was performed by the almighty, about six thousand years ago, before which time the earth was without form and void.

God was six days making the world, and furnishing it with living creatures, and the seventh day he rested from his work, as if he was fatigued.——He made man, the last of all his creatures, the most favored of any, to him he gave dominion over all the reſt——and he called his name Adam.

God now perceived that he had forgotten to make Adam a companion, and that it was not good for him to be alone, ſo he cauſed him to fall into a deep ſleep, took out one of his ribs, and made of it a woman, to be man's companion and helper.— Theſe were created immortal, and lived in a place of infinite beauty and delight:—And God gave them liberty to eat of every thing that grew upon the face of the earth, but of the fruit of one tree, which he prohibited them from taſting upon pain of death.

The man and woman lived together but a little time before a ſerpent addreſſed the woman, and prevailed upon her to break the commands of God, by eating this fruit; which, when ſhe had taſted it, ſhe gave to the man, who did likewiſe eat. The effect of this fruit was to make them know that they were naked.

God coming in the cool of the evening to converſe with Adam, does not immediately find him, therefore calls to him, and, upon receiving an anſwer, aſks him why he did not come to him at firſt? Adam replies, he was aſhamed! becauſe he was naked! God, upon enquiry, then diſcovers, that through the wiles of the ſerpent, they had eaten of the forbidden fruit; he is therefore very angry and curses the serpent, the man, the woman and the whole earth, and drives them out of paradise.

We have afterwards an account of God's sons, who are represented to find the daughters of men so fair as to take them to wife; and soon afterwards the world grows so wicked, that God repents that he had made man, and therefore drowns them all but one man and his family, who, with a pair of every living creature, are preserved in an ark.

The world again becomes full of inhabitants, who forget their God, and act with similar wickedness with those who were before the deluge.

God chuses one people, to whom he particularly declares himself, yet so bad does he seem to have made his choice, that this people are continually acting contrary to his commandments, and are perpetually leaving the worship of God, to join in the sacrifices of the heathen and idolatrous nations.——Many miracles, many signal instances of his power is God stated to have shewn this favored people, yet nothing will prevent their sins.

How surprizing to us doth it appear, when we learn that the man to whom God, according to the bible, first gave authority to write the scriptures, was a murderer:———the man whom he called from a cottage to a palace, was an adulterer.—— the man to whom he gave the greateſt wiſdom, became at laſt an idolator.

Cruelty marks the reigns of almoſt all their kings;— their prophets could not depend upon each other; as murders and crimes of every kind were as frequently committed by the Jews as by the heathen nations. And, notwithſtanding, their prophets were continually exclaiming againſt their ſins, and threatening them with the wrath of the moſt high, yet did they commit offences, even at the inſtant of the exhibition of puniſhment.

The Jews profeſs to believe, that every thing contained in the books of their prophets 1 be fulfilled, and that they are now ſuffering perſecution for their forefathers ſins; but that a king will hereafter be born, who ſhall rule over them with ſplendor, and ſhall reſtore their kingdom to its ancient glory.

The chriſtians, whoſe religion is from the Jews, believe with them in the truth of the bible, but ſay, that the Iſraelites are in an error with reſpect to their expectation of a king: that the perſon who was fore-told by their prophets, has already been upon earth, but that they did not know him in conſequence of having perſuaded themſelves that his kingdom was to be temporal, where

P

as it was strictly spiritual;—this person, the Jews looked upon as an impostor, and destroyed by nailing him upon a cross.

The person thus crucified by the Jews, the christians assert, was no other than the most high God, the creator; who, from before the beginning of the world, foresaw the wickedness and fall of man; and planned his redemption, by a scheme of taking upon himself our flesh, becoming man, and submitting to die upon the cross; this, they contend, was foretold by the Jewish prophets.

The son of God; the son of Man; God himself; the eternal Father; are titles those people give him, and they declare their belief, that there is one God composed of three distinct persons, whom they denominate Father, Son, and Holy Ghost: ———— These three compose but one God, yet are perfectly distinct; and they say, that the trinity in unity, and the unity in trinity is to be worshipped, neither confounding the persons, nor dividing the substance.

They pray to the Father and to the Son equally, yet call the Son the Mediator; they suppose him continually employed in making intercession for mankind, who are every moment offending; yet, at the same time, they say that the sacrifice of his life was accepted by the Father, in full satisfaction for the sins of mankind.

They baptise their children in the name of the Father, Son and Holy Ghost; and believe, that without baptism, they do not receive the benefits of Christ's death.

They affirm that Christ will come again to judge the world; when, although he by his death, made full satisfaction for the sin of Adam, Yet, those who have committed evil will neverthelefs be sent into everlasting fire, while those who have done good will be received into the kingdom of heaven.

The Father, they say is made of none, neither created nor begotten; the son is of the father alone, not made nor created, but begotten; and that he was begotten before the world, yet born in the world. The holy ghost is of the father, and of the son, not made, nor created, nor begotten, but proceeding.

They seem to believe that the Father is generally in heaven, that he made the world and all things by the son, and that the holy ghost is sometimes in heaven, sometimes on earth.

This doctrine of the trinity they call a *myſtery revealed* by God, and although *incomprehenſible*, yet neceſſary to be believed.

Chriſt they ſay is God, yet was begotten, but the father was not begotten; and inſiſt upon the utmoſt credit being given to this, although they confeſs that it is unintelligible.

If you attempt to argue with them, that as according to their opinions, there is but one God, therefore it cannot be improper to worſhip him under any of theſe titles; and as you do not conceive the doctrine of the trinity, God cannot be offended with you, when you addreſs him ſolely as the creator.

To this they reply, that as God has revealed himſelf under the title of Father, Son, and Holy Ghoſt, it is wicked not to believe him.——If you require to know how they prove that this was revealed by God, they ſay it is to be found in the ſcriptures; and they will not ſuffer a doubt of their authenticity.

Chriſt, whom they at all times declare to be the eternal God, at the laſt ſupper of his diſciples, when he deſired them to celebrate it in remembrance of him, took the bread, brake it, and made uſe of theſe words—This is my body!—and when he took the cup, he called the wine, his blood; from hence many chriſtian nations maintain;' that in the communion, the bread is tranſubſtantiated and becomes the very body of Chriſt.

But although this miracle is ſaid to be performed every day by Chriſt, yet, I never heard that he ever produced a miracle, to prove to all men that this was indeed the caſe, which would aſtoniſhingly facilitate the propagation of the goſpel.

According to the accounts of all chriſtian nations, God made man, knowing him to be about to offend him, yet, which man would not do without he ſhould eat of the fruit of a particular tree.

God, inſtead of ſimply deſtroying the tree,—thereby preventing the ſinning of adam.—thereby ſaving thouſands of ſouls from hell fire, and thereby rendering the effect of his own intended ſufferings, ſure and certain in the firſt inſtance—permits the tree to remain—permits man to eat of it—is offended with him for what he knew man could not help—afterwards ſuffers himſelf to be crucified for the redemption of mankind, yet, takes no ſteps to prevent any further wickedneſs from entering the world, which to this day continues to produce wicked men.

These christians seem to have full belief in the pagan power of fate, which was superior to their Gods, and they render the one supreme, as much its subject as were formerly the gods of the heathens; and their priests by preventing the laity from exercising the faculties which God has given them, are enabled to continue them in such a state of confidential blindness, as best answers their interested schemes.

The christians are divided into various sects, who maintain different principles of faith; to their own each gives unlimited assent, and all bring proofs of the truth of their own opinions from the same bible and testament, and likewise from them do they refute the doctrines of the others.———Their teachers contend with great virulence against one another, but none can convince their adversaries; hence we may conclude that the instructions in the bible and testament, which are esteemed by them the particular revelations of God, are not so clear as might be expected to proceed from the omnificient, whose natural laws are so regular and perfect.

The Mahometans, who take their name from their prophet Mahomet, or Mohammed, are of the latest religion that has been formed.

Mahomet lived in the seventh century, P. C. and published his doctrines, as being immediate revelations of God.

He affirmed in oppofition to the Chriftian trinity, that there was but one God, and that himfelf was his prophet.

That Chrift was indeed a teacher fent from God; and that, as mankind would not receive the meek doctrines of Jefus, himfelf was fent by God, with fword and fire, to force mankind to a knowledge of true religion.——Mahomet therefore raifed an army, and put to death whoever refufed to acknowledge him as the prophet of the moft higheft, or who did not receive his writings as the exprefs communications of God.

The koran was written by him, or perhaps by his direction: for one reafon why he commands belief in it, and which he mentions, as a proof of its truth, is, that he, being an unlettered man, could not have compofed fo elegant a work, without aid: the koran bears in many parts, a ftrong refemblance with the bible and Mahomet is faid to have been affifted in forming it by a jew.

Mahomet gives feveral accounts of miraculous events that happened to him, fuch as being carried up into heaven, of whofe diftance he gives a particular account; alfo of the fplendor of the different regions, with the gates and guards that feparate them; all thefe he particularly relates, and delcares, that once he had a great many thoufands converfations with God, yet the time he was gone from the earth was so short, that when he returned, his bed was not cold, nor was all the water run out of a pitcher, that stood by his bed-side, and was thrown down by the animal, which carried him to God.

The people Mahomet was among were much addicted to sensual pleasures, and therefore, in his description of paradise, he painted those delicious, luxurious scenes, which he knew would captivate his followers, and he composed his whole religion upon the same principles.

Himself was much addicted to women, but, his adulteries becoming offensive to the people, he wrote a particular chapter of the koran, as from God, authorising his prophet to indulge himself in every gratification.

Mahometanism is a mixture of judaism and christianity, joined with such doctrines as Mahomet perceived would be necessary, to accomplish his ambitious designs;——and his plan succeeded so well, that he raised himself, almost miraculously, from a very low station, to the highest that human nature can possibly fill.

From the examination of these principal religions, it is certain that God is not rightly known, by most of the inhabitants of the world; for if we look to the God of Mahomet, we see him delighting in cruelty and punishing in the commonality offences which he permits to his favourite.

If to the God of the jews, a Being of all power and fore-knowledge, condemning a creature whom he had formed immortal to death for yielding to a temptation which he had purposely put in his way; angry, yet forgiving; proud and jealous, yet merciful;—just, yet changing his judgment,—chusing one people as a favoured nation, to whom he might reveal himself; yet do we find his people putting less confidence in him, than the heathen nations do in their idols.

If to the God of the christians, a Being of infinite perfection, determining from all eternity to form a creature, whose wickedness he foresaw would be so great, as to be no otherways done away, except by himself lowering his divine nature, and submitting to death. And this he is said to have done; yet man has not been freed from sin, for his children are to this moment transgressing, and are equally imperfect as they were before this sacrifice.

DISCOURSE the THIRD.

In the lesson we read this morning, we found these words.

"But as for me and my House, we will serve the Lord."

If there is any subject that demands the particular attention of mankind, it is religion.

Religion arises from the ideas we have of a superior Being, and means the worship which we think ourselves bound to pay to him; but unless we have proper ideas of this Being, the services that we intend to render to him, will necessarily be unworthy of him.

O Almighty God, who knowest the hearts of men, and art alone the judge of the motives to our actions; look with favor on thy humble servant, who wishes to exert the faculties thou hast given him towards gaining such a knowledge of thee, as will make him more able and more desirous to fulfil thy will in all things.————Thou seest into all his designs; thou art sensible of the exalted ideas he has of thy nature; thou knowest the prejudices he may have to come.—— Enable him, O Lord! humbly to seek thy kingdom;

and not putting any implicit faith in the opinions of man, but trusting solely in thee, grant that he may be able to see through the clouds and darkness, which overshadow the earth! and that he may know, and fear, and serve thee the only God, to thy glory, and to the happiness of all thy creatures upon earth. Amen.

This day, my friends, I intend to deliver to you some reflections extracted from my manuscripts, which I wrote before I left England; and which will explain to you the ideas that I had upon religious subjects:—I shall make no alterations, because they were written when my mind was filled with the persuasion that the world was in an error; and you will perceive from them, in what manner it seemed to free itself from the prejudices of education.

The christian religion is that in which I was brought up, I admire its instructions; I hope I am a true christian:———but I cannot approve or assent to all the doctrines of our teachers, and I doubt of many of their most material tenets.

The bible and testament I cannot look upon as being immediately from God;———We learn from history, the council which sanctioned the latter;———we likewise are informed that there were other gospels besides those of the four Evangelists;——if they were written by inspiration, what authority had the council to reject any?——But the gospels are evidently the works of men;—corrected and selected by men;——and as they admit of miracles, let me ask whether any miracle has been performed to prove that they are entirely approved of by the Almighty? ¶ During my life, I have seen no personal interposition of providence;——I do not look upon the whole earth of sufficient consequence to require it.———Generally immutable laws are every where evident to me, and altho' my senses are limited, my ideas scarce know a boundary.

All space appears full of the greatness of my God. Worlds beyond worlds!—Systems beyond systems! innumerable myriads of creations appear in the mirror of my eye; I feel the majesty of the omnipotent, and I exclaim, O Lord! what is man?—A wonderful being as a creature, but still of very small consequence in comparison with the rest of creation!

Persuaded as I am of the greatness of God; of the insignificance of man; and of there being numberless other worlds; can I readily give my assent to a tale, which I am told, that the son of God, God himself, came down from heaven to visit mankind; to experience our nature; to take upon himself our flesh; to suffer death for to cleanse mankind from their sins?—— I cannot.

The doctrine of the divinity of Christ is not implicitly to be believed:—If Christ was the eternal God, a strict examination will prove to his glory; and without having duly examined it, the professors of this belief, whenever they make this declaration of faith, offer insult instead of honor to that august Being, who, they say, took upon himself our flesh.

It appears an improbability; it does not come home to my reason to admit, that my God should deign to visit the earth in a human form;——but supposing, for a moment, that he should, this do I feel convinced of, that his condescension must have the greatest end in view:——That the means employed by him would be the best that could be devised,—and that the effect would be certain:

When I ask the motive of his coming upon earth? The answer is, to save the world. As man, I acknowledge the design to be great and momentous.——I enquire how he accomplished it? By shewing himself upon earth as man,——telling the jews of their sins, preaching a future immortal state, where punishments and rewards were prepared,—setting an example of perfect life, offering himself up as a sacrifice for sin, and yielding up his life upon a cross.———To whom does he offer up this sacrifice? to God.——But it is said that Christ is the sole omnipotent being,—that himself and the father are as one—if so, what was the value of the sacrifice?— it was nothing! for God cannot die;——if Christ was God, his death was a deception.

But granting that he was the Lord God omnipotent; granting that he did die;——Let me ask, must not this sacrifice have been ample? assuredly— could God have been deceived in the effect? certainly not.——What then has been the advantage?——Are men restored to their immortality?— Is sin taken away from the world? no,—men are still wicked, and still yield up their lives to death.

Do even all men know these doctrines? are they now more studious to do the will of God?——We preach against their impieties, and thereby fully answer the question.

Did God come to save the world in general, or only a particular part?——If in general the facts appear, he came so like a man, that few could tell the difference, and even his chief disciple denied him in the hour of danger.———— He shewed himself to but one people, and but for a short space of time: he suffered this people to doubt of his divinity, and at length to prove his mortality, by absolutely killing him. Now we are told, that he has threatened them with punishment for not believing that he was God, even when they had seen him die;———How inferior to my ideas of God!

If miracles are to prove the interference of the deity, their effect cannot be futile.———————God cannot be mistaken; they must be necessary, and must produce the destined end.————If God had come upon earth to save all mankind, he certainly would not have concealed himself from the greater part of the universe; and if he expected belief in himself, he would have prevented the possibility of doubt, by making himself known to all nations; which miraculous effect of the divine power, would have been worthy the greatness and goodness of our God, and all mankind would have been benefited by it.

But to say, that God himself came down from heaven, took upon himself our nature, bore our infirmities, suffered death for our sakes, yet permitted $\frac{999+}{1000+}$ parts of the world to be ignorant of his being upon earth, no ways accords with my ideas of the omnipotent. That he should fail in rendering mankind more virtuous, appears to me, likewise an improbability, and I am induced to conclude, that the title of the fole God, being given to Chrift, is a clear and certain corruption of man.

I read the fcriptures, I admire the doctrines therein contained, and that which I believe to be the religion which Chrift wifhed to eftablifh, receives my fulleft affent, and my reafon approves of it;—— I acknowledge its beauty, its fimplicity.—and I lament that the effect which it would have, if truly preached, is deftroyed thro' the fuperftructures of ignorant or defigning men.———It gives us juft notions of God; and his attributes, of man's duties to God; to his neighbour and himfelf: and the morality which Chrift preached would, if duly practifed, be productive of happinefs, both in this world, and in that which is to come.

By fome perfons it may be efteemed prefumptuous, to fay that man can form any idea of the intentions of God in the creation of the world; but I am perfuaded, that if his reafon were properly exerted, the difcoveries which he is able to make, would appear incredible to thofe, who have been bred up in the fear of ufing the powers, which yet they believe themfelves to poffefs.

God has furely given me reafon, in order that I fhould ufe it, and I am determined to exercife it in a free examination of all things, until my Heavenly Father shall prove to me his disapprobation, by not permitting me to have clear ideas of that which I seek, but which he does not chuse that I should know.

I will look into the histories of the world, the writings and opinions of the different nations——I will combine the ideas which I receive, and will freely declare those truths of which I am convinced.

It is clear that there is a God;—every thing proves it;—the more we examine into nature, the more we are convinced of his wisdom and power.

The animated world is a regular chain of improving creatures, and forms a most admirable work.——This system of revolving orbs, to which our earth belongs, still further proves the greatness of our Creator, and we even cannot doubt of a God.

What then is man? — An animal endued with reason.

What is Reason?——A faculty whereby we are enabled either to combine or separate the ideas which our animal senses convey to us; and also to form new combinations that may produce ideas which are not the objects of the animal senses.

R

Have we any innate ideas?—None; all our ideas arife from fenfation, reflection, and communication; we are therefore juftified in cautioufly examining any new idea; and we may either give our affent or may object to it, according to the conviction which we feel of its being true or falfe.

God made the world, and all that it contains;—as he was not under an indifpenfible neceffity of doing it, 'tis clear his own will was alone confulted. And, finding every thing provided for the happinefs of the creature, we readily affent to the doctrine, that God in his plan willed, that his creatures fhould be happy.

We fee unhappinefs in the world, we wonder that God fhould fuffer it; but upon examining further, we find it to be a neceffary confequence of that free agency which God has chofen to permit his creatures to enjoy, and which his immutability will not fuffer him to revoke. Man is thereby made to inflict upon himfelf the punifhment that his follies have deferved.

We know but little of the firft ages of the world.—The memory of a man is but a bad repofitory for events, and his mind is a book which is liable to continual error: thus may we juftly fuppofe, that no tradition was ever handed through feveral generations without alteration or addition;—the fon's opinion, in fome inftances, differed perhaps from the father's, and he related to his children that which he thought was right; but when writing was invented, then was a new fenfe given to man. But the art at firft was confined to a very few, and manufcripts were in the poffeffion of a fmall number of perfons.

From this want of true accounts has arifen different opinions of the time of the creation of the world, fome people fixing it thoufands of years before others.—The account which we have in our Bible of this event, is a fine defcription, but upon examining it we fhall find it fo unphilofophical, that we fhall be under the neceffity of attributing it to the ftrength of Mofes' imagination, rather than to the revelation of God.

Could we paint to ourfelves all fpace in confufion, and the Omnipotent as if waking out of a dream, determining to make a univerfe merely for the fake of man, we might give credit to the relation of the lights of heaven being made the fourth day; but when aftronomical obfervations prove to us the real fize of the fun and ftars, and hiftory convinces us of the ignorance of former ages, who can help exclaiming, correct thyfelf, thou new enlightened creature! Far be it from thee to affert that God made thefe folely for thy ufe.——Thou canft no where difcover another fuch ufelefs exertion of power!

'God is the God of all; his wisdom, his greatness, and his power, are without bounds. From the discoveries which we, in these later ages, have made, by the assistance of instruments, which have given new senses unto us, enabling us more clearly to know the works of our creator, we are convinced that those orbs which our fore-fathers supposed were made for enlightning the earth, are, in reallity, other worlds, subjected to revolutions similar to our world. Nor is it absurd to suppose them to be filled with living creatures, who partake of the bounty of their God.

All nature acknowledges a supreme:—his goodness is visible throughout all his works.—How admirably adapted is every thing for accomplishing whatever is expected from it!

When I look upon an anatomized animal, how forcibly do I feel the certainty of a God! How wonderful!—What art!—What beauty!—What inimitable perfection!—How wonderfully distinct, how wonderfully combined!

Surely I will seek my God—Nor shall man prevent me from the free use of my reason:—God knows it is not presumptuously I say so, but hereby am I persuaded that I best prove my title to the name of man.

Is God the object of our animal senses?—Not immediately. Is he discoverable by our reason?—In a small degree he is. Is the idea of God innate?—It does not seem to be so. God then has created beings who may be ignorant of him?—Yes. How do you know that there is a God?—Because every thing that is the object of my senses is an effect. Reason informs me no effect can take place without a cause; the first cause I call God, who is necessary self-existent, and I believe that God is a perfect being.

It may be asked whether a perfect being would form so imperfect a creature as man?——The question is founded in error, man's nature is perfect, that is, as of a man, although it be imperfect as of a God.

The imperfections and unhappiness which we find among mankind are not to be ascribed to God, but to the misuse of the powers he has given us; for he has provided all his creatures with the means of rendering their situations pleasing.

God is all-wise, and hence are his decrees immutable; this is every day proved to us, by those occurrences which are unnoticed, solely from our being used to them.

The sun shines alike upon the virtuous and wicked;—the rain refreshes all lands;—the seasons return;—the years revolve;—the good and the bad pay equally the debt of nature.——Creatures are born and die ; and the world knows no change of the regular ordination, which we found when we entered upon it ; our old men speak of none but natural effects ; God is the same from everlasting, and his goodnefs is feen in all his works.

Did men exert their reafon, how differently would many things appear to them to what they now do!— But in this are they to be pitied, for parents breed up their children in the prejudices of the nation in which they are born ! The eftablifhed religion of moft countries forbids them to doubt of its truth, or to freely examine its principles ; and declares that faith in the revelations of God is abfolutely neceffary for falvation, which faith is only proved by an unlimited confidence.

Yet do I find many different nations declaring, that they have received the particular revelations of God ; when upon comparing them, I difcover that thefe revelations are contradictory, even in material parts. Can I believe the one God can act fo much beneath himfelf ? Can God be equally changeable as man ?

Doth God command one people to kneel to the crofs, and direct another to trample on it ? Doth he tell one nation that his Paradife is furnifhed for the moft exquifite fenfual delights ? while to another he declares that fenfuallity is difpleafing to him ?

All thefe cannot be the revelations of God; and without making ufe of my reafon, how can I difcriminate the right?—Can my being born at Mecca, make God a different Being from the God of the Chriftians?—God cannot change, he is always the fame; alike good, beneficent, and attentive to the prayers of the humble and meek.

I agree, that whatfoever God declares to me, muft be true, and no doubt can remain with me, but that I ought to perform whatever commands he lays upon me. But then let me fay, when what is called the will of God is declared to me by man, that although I do acknowledge myfelf bound to do his will, yet have I full liberty to enquire, and indeed it is my duty to examine, whether that which others declare to me as the will of God, is fo or not. Indeed all thofe who believe in the authority of the bible, muft acknowledge the force of this argument by their own ftory of the prophet who was deftroyed by the lion.

Shall a man have unlimited confidence becaufe he daringly prefumes to fay, I have feen God, who has ordered me to command you to believe the things which I now tell you? Belief, God knows is uncontroulable.—I cannot doubt, and therefore I believe. It is not becaufe I wifh to believe that therefore I do, but truely becaufe I cannot believe otherwife.

No man, really coming from God, would say, you *must* believe what I tell you. All he could say would be this——What I relate to you, I assure you I had from God, who commanded me to declare it unto you, that you *may* know his will and fulfill it.

Hence I claim a right to examine what is denominated revelation, and I look upon myself particularly called upon, to acquaint myself with the truth of the religion in which I was brought up, and to examine with humble freedom, the truth of the grand principle that **Christ** indeed was the very God.

God has evidently left the mind of man free, and although he made it capable of reasoning, and of exerting its powers to the true sublime, by unprejudicedly reflecting on the objects that surround it; yet it was not his design to force mankind to exceed their natures, or even to compel them to use the faculties which he hath given them.

I do suppose that God implanted in the first man just ideas of his greatness and power, and having blessed him with all necessary knowledge, passed an unalterable decree, that man should be a free agent.

We know in these later days, how easily corruption pervades mental tradition; and, from our own experience of the effects to be expected from uncultivated reason, we need not greatly wonder at mankind lofing all juft ideas of God.—Their animal nature overwhelmed their fpiritual : In a few ages they looked for their God among his works, and worfhipped the Creator under the form of the creature; till afterwards a worfe corruption followed—for they worfhipped the creature as God.

Still the nature of man remained the fame; the fiat of God had gone forth, and was immutable:—His goodnefs bore with his creatures infirmities, and fparing the vengeance he might have juftly inflicted, he left them to experience the calamities which their own follies would bring upon them.

One people, according to their own accounts, retained a knowledge of the true God; but their religion was filled with ceremonials, and their hearts would hardly own the great I AM; they worfhipped him as the God of juftice; yet fanctioned their own cruelties under the pretended mandates of the Father of Mercies.

Prophets were confulted by Jews, and oracles by Idolators; to both was fometimes permitted the foreknowledge of future events.——A fupreme preferver of the world was believed by all nations; and the true God might at all times have been known by that mind which was capable of getting the better of the prejudices of edu-

S

cation;—but to produce an unprejudiced mind appears almost a miracle.

In Jesus Christ, we are justified in saying, that this was discoverable; he had a just idea of the majesty of the King of Heaven; he saw through the impiety of offering up sacrifices for sin, while the heart remained uncleansed.—The fasts and new moons of the Jews his soul abhorred; he saw through their wickedness; he lamented the depraved state of mankind; he burned to declare the true God, and to make his name revered throughout all nations.

Wishing to make known the great Creator, in order that his people might be induced to correct the errors which debased them, the blessed Jesus commenced his scheme by acquainting himself with the opinions of the Hebrew Doctors; and at twelve years old we find him consulting with them in the temple.

The Evangelists have not given us that minute account of the early years of Christ which might have been expected; But had he been the Creator himself, as the Christians maintain, no one moment could have passed without being of consequence to mankind; nor would he have suffered one action to escape him without its being faithfully recorded.

Would the omnifcient God, who thus is fuppofed to have made an alteration in the fyftem which he had planned; who, it is faid, took upon himfelf our flefh; fuffered himfelf to be nailed to the crofs; died for our redemption; that is, to redeem us from his own anger—Would this kind, this beneficent Being, who thus interefted himfelf in the welfare of man, have gone from the earth without preventing mankind from having a doubt of his divinity? Would he not have left with all future ages a certainty which they could not have difputed? This would have been a miracle worthy of our God! By fuch an act, his intention of coming upon earth would have been anfwered! He would truly have made himfelf known to all nations, and we might each of us have faid to our children, this is the Lord's own act! Doubt it if you can!

But what is the fact? — Jefus chofe fimple low born men to be his companions, becaufe his own fituation in life was low, his father Jofeph being a carpenter; they were witneffes of his purity and of his virtues; they faw him all beneficent; they loved him; he taught them his doctrines; they were convinced of his truth, and they believed in him.

When he began his miniftry, he preached to the people of the goodnefs of God; of his love for his works, of his wifhes for them properly to exert the powers which he had given them; of the neceffity of avoiding fin, and the benefit to be hoped from sincere repentance.——He taught them, that the God of mercies had planned every thing for the happiness of his creatures; that all that God had required from them was, to act in such a manner as would promote the welfare of each other, and to be thankful to their God for his merciful kindness. He told them that God would not suffer wilful misconduct, which tended to oppress the meanest of his creatures, to go unpunished; nor had he intended that the unhappiness which the free agency of man might produce, should be without alleviation; but as this world could not be the seat of rewards and punishments, without counteracting his pre-determined unalterable plans, he gave them to believe in a future immortal state.—This I believe to be the religion of Jesus.

Warmed with the conscious justness of his thoughts; sensible of the consequence they were of to mankind; he determined to boldly declare them before the face of all people.—Low in station, of no weight in the councils of the city, but filled with the love of God, Jesus firmly commenced his teaching.

Truth wants not the assistance of art.—Jesus declares to the people the true God; he tells them, in the simplest manner, their vices and their duties;—he explains how unwelcome to the purity of God, were their fastiduous religious ceremonials ; and proving by his humility, his virtue, his univerfal benevolence, and his fteady refufal of temporary honours, that no other motive but contributing to the glory of God and the happinefs of mankind had urged him to action ; he feeks for every opportunity of encreafing the number of the virtuous.

The love of God, proved by love to mankind, was what he required from his hearers. He taught with confidence ; he cenfured with mildnefs and compaffion ; but his foul was oftentimes afflicted, and he wept for the obduracy of his fellow creatures.

Thus preaching in truth, and fetting an example of virtuous living, did the bleffed Jefus pafs his life.—The Jewifh people began to fee the darknefs which had overfhadowed them ; they looked to the light with admiration; they wondered at their teacher ; they thought him worthy, they wifhed him to be their king ; they trufted, he was the perfon whom they expected about this time, who, as foretold by their prophets, would enable them to throw off the Roman yoke.

But Jefus refufed their honours ; his object was different; he wanted to call mankind to a knowledge of the true God, and in accomplifhing this lay all his ambition.

Numbers now fought him; they followed him, they adored him; they called him good;—but Jesus is said to have answered, " why callest thou me good? there is none good but one, that is God." All his discourses breathe that exalted piety and respect to the most high, which none but a Being of his virtue could attain;—He was surely the beloved of God!

Fully acquainted with the writings of the ancient prophets, he seemed to believe a Messias would appear who should instruct Israel in the knowledge of the true God. He found himself strongly impelled to take upon himself the ministry; but when John sent for to ask, " Art thou he that should come, or do we look for another?" His humility would not suffer him to assume that high office—if he was the person foretold by the prophets, he knew that the Lord was true: but whether the prophecy was fulfilled in him, he did not presume to say, but answered, " Go and shew John those things which ye do hear and see;" that is, I do not say I am the Messias, but my works must prove whether I am or not.

When, in the 16th chapter of Saint Matthew, Jesus enquires of his disciples whom they suppose that he is? Simon Peter answers, Thou art the Christ, the son of the living God;—Jesus answers, " Blessed art thou, for flesh and blood hath not revealed it to thee, but my Father which is in Heaven.

If he was the Chrift, he knew that Peter muft be a worthy difciple, becaufe the Almighty had firft communicated it to him; and knowing the worth of Peter, he doubts not his truth; thus being perfuaded that he might be the perfon fpoken of by the prophets, he fhews to his difciples the fufferings which he muft experience, and declares more openly to them the meaning of the fcriptures; but knowing that his actions would alone prove the truth of his miffion, he forbids them that they tell any man he was the Chrift.—— He encourages them in virtue, and he comforts them with the hopes of a happy reft through the mercies of God :—This feems to be the true ftatement, as collected from the Teftament.

The chiefs of the Jewifh fynagogue perceiving, from the number of thofe who followed him every day encreafing, that their interefts were leffening, ftudied to entangle him by queftions of the greateft fubtility; but Jefus returned their queftions upon them, and refufed to tell them the authority by which he preached. He declared how much the Almighty Father was difpleafed at the pretended religion of the Scribes and Pharifees, and affured them that the unexpreffed real forrow of the heart, was more efficacious in wafhing away fin, than all the oblations and facrifices of the Jewifh ritual.

Unable to convict him of error, they faw no way of preferving their confequence, but by deftroying Jefus, and they council'd to put him to death.

This world was not defired by Jefus; he looked with confidence to a future ftate; he knew their confpiracies, but he knew, that without the permiffion of God, they could not hurt him; he believed himfelf fent on earth to call mankind to a knowledge of their God,—he was perfuaded that he acted under a divine impulfe, and was all fubmiffion to the divine will.

He avoided not the betrayer;—he was bound and lead to judgment;——Pilate afked him—Art thou the king of the Jews?——Jefus anfwered, thou fayft.

I cannot fay I could ever underftand this reply,—for it conveys no clear idea to me; and however proper it might be in the man Jefus not to anfwer any enfnaring queftion, I am convinced no fuch reafon could actuate the God of nature.)

The evening he was betrayed, his foul was exceeding forrowful, even unto death; and he prayed 'O my Father! if it be poffible: let this cup pafs from me; neverthelefs, not as I will, but as thou wilt,' and a fecond time he prayed, 'O my Father! if this cup may not pafs away from me, except I drink it, thy will be done;' and he went a third time and prayed, faying the fame words.

What a mockery is here if Jefus was the God of creation! he prays to himfelf, yet will not grant his own prayer; three times does he befeech himfelf to avoid death, yet cannot do it—'tis abfurd!

But how changed is the fcene, when we behold this a conflict between the body and foul of a virtuous man; how beautiful! how fublime!

Knowing that his end approached, yet lamenting the ignorance in which his fellow creatures were ftill involved, the bleffed Jefus hoped, if the Almighty would delay the period of his death, that he might be able to encreafe the true believers, and that the other nations of the earth might be taught the knowledge of the true God: But as it was not given him to judge contrary to the will of his Heavenly Father, and confiding, that his ordinances would be for the beft, he expreffes his refignation and willingnefs to fuffer death, if fo it feemed fit to his God.

This is the greateft trial of the faith of man; Jefus proved his truth, by fubmiting to the death of the crofs.

No reply did he make to the fcoffs of the ignorant multitude; he was nailed to the crofs, in full confidence of having done his duty; yet it fhould feem he had hoped that, before his death, God would have given an indubitable proof of his innocence. For finding himfelf perifhing without any appearance of fuch interpofition, he feared that God had forfaken him; and he exclaimed, " My God, my God, why haſt thou forſaken me :" but the Almighty ſuffered him to pay the debt of nature, in order as it ſeems, to make Chriſt's nature quite clear, and to prevent, as far as his immutable laws would permit, the diſciples and poſterity from having the erroneous opinion, of Chriſt himſelf being the divine firſt cauſe, which might have been the caſe had he permitted him to aſcend immediately from the croſs into heaven.

Yet to convince mankind of the truth of Chriſt, he, according to the Chriſtian tradition, rent the vail of the temple in twain, from top to bottom; he commanded the ſun to be darkened, the graves to be opened, and the bodies of the ſaints to appear unto many: Thus ended the life of Chriſt. He was buried; but his body did not remain in the ſepulchre; the Evangeliſts declare he aroſe again the third day, and aſcended into heaven—the Jews ſay the body was ſtolen.— Of early reported tranſactions, God alone can tell what is the truth.

It is ſufficient for us, that Jeſus lived, taught the knowledge of the true God in purity and truth, ſet us an indubitable example of virtue, and died to prove his faith. It becomes us, in all things, to conduct ourſelves in ſuch a manner as will be agreeable to God; this Jeſus commanded; to this our reaſon aſſents, and the commandments of the Almighty ought to be engraven in our hearts.

If ye aſk what are the commandments of God? take this anſwer:

There is but one God—Ye ſhall have no other Gods but him—His name ſhall be ever reſpected, and ye ſhall worſhip no other—The relative duties ye ſhall not neglect; your own happineſs is involved in that of others; for no wilful injury ſhall be unnoticed, or in its event deſirable.

May we all think worthily of God! Of that majeſtic ſupreme who has bleſſed us with reaſon, whereby we may know him! May our hearts be warmed with the love of him, who has permitted us to perceive his univerſal love for his creatures.—He is the fame for ever and ever.—Bleſſed be the Lord God of Heaven! May his name be known through all the earth! And may the lives of all his people be evermore conducted according to his will!

And, at the name of Jeſus, let us look up to heaven with raptures, and let affection and reſpect be felt in every breaſt; for it was he who firſt broke through the darkneſs of idolatry, and preached the Lord God Omnipotent in purity and truth!

His victory let us glory in; for he conquered the fears of Death and the terrors of the grave!—His life was an example of the higheſt virtue ;—his death was a proof of his belief in God.——He cleanſed the temple from impurities; he made manifeſt the God of nature; he lived free from ſin, and died in righteouſneſs; and we may now juſtly exclaim, O Death, where is thy ſting? O Grave, where is thy victory? Bleſſed be the Lord God Omnipotent, who has given us the victory!

DISCOURSE the FOURTH.

BRETHREN, we will, this morning, turn our thoughts to confider thofe motives of our governor Jacobus, which induced him to leave his country, and the religion of his fathers, and at length to form the laws of this country, upon the foundation of what he was convinced, was truly the will of God.

JACOBUS VERITAS was born in England, and was brought up in what is called the Church of England, to diftinguifh it from other Proteftant congregations, which are fo called from their protefting againft the doctrines of the Church of Rome.—The people of England, in emancipating themfelves from the Romifh Church, ftill retain feveral of its prejudices; but the toleration allowed in that country is favourable to the free enquirer.

Jacobus, in the early part of his life, was exceedingly fond of philofophical refearches, and from thence was convinced of the certainty of One great firft caufe.— Taught from his infancy to have a high veneration for the Deity; he wifhed, when his mental faculties encreafed, to gain a clear and diftinct knowledge of him:— but the writers whom he confulted, in general connected what was fatisfactory to reafon with what was fo totally contrary to it, that he felt within his breast an uneasiness of which he cou'd not get the better. Either his ideas of God were very erroneous, and he must be obnoxious to God's anger; or else if his thoughts were true, the greater part of the world was in an error.—He sought the opinions of all nations, and not one of them was satisfactory unto him: he brought them all together, and found so much difference between them, that he thought himself justified in rejecting them all; and from his own reason, to form a system of religion according to what he thought was right.

He perceived that religion seemed to depend absolutely on the place of birth:——That in one part of Europe men knelt to the cross, while in another they trampled upon it; that in some parts, they esteemed it a damnable offence to doubt whether God did come upon earth to die for man, that in others, the confession of this faith was thought an absurdity.

Convinced that there is but one God, and therefore, that two or more distinct ideas of him, could not proceed from his own revelation; he determined to search, whether, in any of the prevailing religions of the world, there were the evident marks of a revelation from God.

Three he found most general,—Jewish, Mahometan, and Christian."

The first, the clergy of England treated as a wilful continuance in error; the second as an impious imposture; but Jacobus perceived that the people who confessed those two religions were more numerous than the christians; and when the Heathen and other nations were joined with them, that the proportion of the Christians was very small; and therefore, assenting to the truth of a doctrine of his church, that every soul was of equal consequence in the eyes of God; he could not readily believe that God would permit such a number, ignorantly to incur the sentence of damnation.

He learnt, that the Mahometan nations believed that God had published his will in the Koran: This book Jacobus procured, but was soon convinced of the impostor, and easily discovered the ambitious policy of Mahomet; while the great Alla was represented more like a king of the earth than of heaven. Mahomet's description of the celestial regions being entirely composed of the valuables of the earth, and diamonds and other jewels sparkling with glorious lustre.

His paradise is filled with scenes of gay delight; and beautiful women, with luscious wines are held out as rewards for those who die in Mahometanism; this surely could not be the revelation of God!

Christianity, founded on judaism, called his attention, and he found its professors declaring, that the bible was written by the immediate infpiration of God, and therefore, that in this and the teftament, was to be difcovered every article of faith.

The bible begins with fuch an account of the formation of the world as foon fatisfied him God was not the author of it; and from the contradictions and abfurdities which are in many parts of it, he faw, too vifibly, another work of man attempted to be forced on mankind, as the word of the fupreme.

He renounced the opinion, that God had given the bible and teftament for the fole guides of mankind; and he looked into his own breaft, for new principles to go upon: He took as Data.

That there is one felf exiftent Being, or God, who created all things: And that this Being is of infinite perfection and goodnefs.

Man, then he acknowledged a creature, made by God; he knew that an all-wife and all-powerful Being would create every thing proper for the completion of his purpofe;———But what his purpofe was, could not be known by the creature, unlefs God gave him faculties to perceive it.

Filled with the moſt exalted ideas of God, and finding the powers of reaſon to have been a gift from him, he ventured to aſſert, that nothing which was incompatible with the ideas which his reaſon gave him of the goodneſs and greatneſs of his God, could proceed, by Revelation, from the ſupreme.

The creation is ſurely a proof of the greatneſs, wiſdom, and power of the moſt high; but the account which is given in the Bible, of the fall of man, is unworthy of the God of mercy.

To ſuppoſe, that man was framed, in his firſt earthly ſtate, immortal, is a thought which no reaſonable mind can allow; for it would be admitting, as a faƈt, that which every hour contradiƈts. And if, according to the chriſtian teachers, the omniſcient God foreſaw man would eat of the forbidden fruit, and that he himſelf muſt die to redeem the world; he muſt alſo have known, that even his dying would not prevent mankind from continuing in ſin; and that there was one ſimple and efficacious way of preventing the wickedneſs of man, viz. deſtroying the tree that produced this fruit, but this he would not do.——God thus is made to conſent to the damnation and eternal puniſhment of creatures, who could not avoid offending him: For the fore-knowledge of God, can only proceed from his power of ordering future events.

U

In the testament, Jacobus found fine moral ideas, and a more worthy account of God, than in any other of the Jewish or Heathen writings.——Christ, he perceived, must have declared the true God in purity; but that his simple intelligible doctrines, adapted to the understanding and benefit of all men were so obscured, by those who delivered them to posterity, that at length, the religion which Christ preached, in a simple and clear manner, viz. ' Thou shalt love the Lord thy God with ' all thy heart, and him only shalt thou serve'; and ' thy neighbour thou shalt love as thyself' was filled, with unintelligible and extraordinary opinions.

Jacobus set about clearing all the superstitious superstructures which he found added to the religion of Jesus; and he has left us the pure doctrines of that virtuous person.

He saw that the errors of mankind arose, from not exerting their own faculties, but trusting, with implicitness to others;—this he used to shew, was alluded to by the condemnation of the servant who hid his talent in a napkin, as we read in the testament; and he strictly enjoined us all: ' To doubt whoever shall tell you, ' that ye must not trust to, and use, the talent of reason ' which God has given you.——Ye cannot, with the ' utmost efforts of your power, discover any thing which

'God does not will you to perceive; and the more that
'ye freely enquire into his effence, the more will ye be
'convinced of his truth.'

Doubt that there is God if ye can! may be faid to every one who will unprejudicedly, or indeed, even prejudicedly employ his talents in the examination of nature.

From the fituation of man, it will appear, that there muft be three duties which he has to perform; his duty to God; his duty to his neighbour; and his duty to himfelf;——thefe three are fo intimately connected, that one cannot be omitted without the others being broken through.

Our duty to God, is defcribed by all nations, to confift, in believing him,—fearing him, loving him,—puting our whole truft in him, and calling upon him.

But to accomplifh this, it will be neceffary to exercife our reafon, in order to enable us to have proper ideas of our God.

There have been men who have faid with their mouths they did not believe there was a God: A fimple, but forcible argument may be held with such men.—If there be no Creator, man is either self-formed, or the production of chance; (tho' none of them can explain what they mean;) to one or other they will agree:— Let then man's body be chained to the ground, his hands and feet fastened, and let this Being be laid in a dungeon, without food;—when either himself, or chance shall release him, ack..wledge that you will be convinced by the experiment; which none of them, I believe, would venture to make, because they would see that there was no chance in the case.

There is a God, our Creator! although not perceptable by our senses, which are only adapted to the clear comprehension of those things that are necessary to us in our present state of existence.

To believe in him, is in some degree, an act of necessity in a thinking mind; for the more we exert the powers which he has given us, the more are we satisfied that there is a God. When we examine the art, the contrivance that is, discoverable in the minutest thing upon earth; when following the idea, we trace the first appearance, the state of perfection; and afterwards the declining state of every thing living, till at length it returns to earth: when we go beyond this world, and admire the sun, the luminous centre of our planetary system, and afterwards permit our minds to range to that part of space, where are the fixed stars, which we readily believe to be other worlds: what poffibility have we to avoid a belief in God?

To fear him,—to love him, muft be the effects of a proper belief in him; and thefe are fo ftrongly impreffed upon the mind which knoweth God, that there is not one inftance to the contrary.

God does not feem to have given us any innate ideas; not even of himfelf. When he created the world, and called man into exiftence, he might perhaps have given by infpiration, that which after ages were to poffefs only by application.

To enquire how long the world has been, is a fpeculation of little ufe; but the examination of the ftate in which it is at the period of our exifting in it, is a neceffary and proper enquiry; and by applying to our reafon, we fhall be enabled to know what is right for us to do.

Truft to no man's opinion in thofe things wherein yourfelves are concerned: But by reading and difcourfe endeavour to convince your own reafon, and act in ftrict conformity to that which yourfelves are perfuaded is right.

God has evidently made men free agents, and has not abfolutely hindered them from being guilty of actions that difgrace their nature; but upon examining into fuch as are thus guilty, we fhall find them either quite ignorant of God, or elfe poffeffing very erroneous ideas of him.

God is omnifcient and omnipotent! Was man fully perfuaded of this, would he wilfully offend a Being, who could punifh him, when at the fame time, he knew that he could not conceal his tranfgreffion from him?

It is from ignorance of God, that fo many vices and fins are committed; for many men talk much about God, who, by their actions, prove they have not known him.

Whatever injury is committed againft man, is an offence that cannot be agreeable to God; and from hence, has been derived, one of the proofs of a future ftate of rewards and punifhments; becaufe many virtuous men fuffer, while wicked men feem to profper in the world; and therefore it is hoped that God will render that juftice in a future ftate, which he omits in the prefent.

Thefe things appear dark to us, nor will they be cleared up, till our fouls are freed from their earthly habitation; then shall our faculties be enabled to discover what God has appointed; and we may hope, that our knowledge will be perfected.

To put our trust in God, and to call upon him, are necessary effects of a just knowledge of him; for conscious of his own weakness, and convinced of the power of his God, what man can refrain from trusting in him and calling upon him?

The duty of calling upon God is so much of the nature of a high favour and permission, that a man ought to be fearful of becoming unworthy of it, and losing it.

Prayer to God is a duty which his creatures are bound to fulfil for their own interest; but the prayers to which God attends are not mere forms of words, but the sincere petitions which proceed from the heart.—The man who prays sincerely, is he who studies to acquaint himself with his God, and whose actions are the result of his desire to fulfil the end for which he was called into being.—'Tis not the impenitent hypocrite who comes into church, says his prayers, and goes from thence to the immediate commission of vice, that will receive the blessings which he asks; but he, who conscious of his own weakness, humbly beseeches remission of his God for his past offences, prays for strength to avoid transgressing for the future, and studiously avoids being guilty of any fin.——It is not he who calls Lord! Lord! that shall enter into the kingdom of heaven, but he alone who doeth the will of God.

Chrift has left us a form of prayer the moft fimple and comprehenfive imaginable, and has declared the folly of long hypocritical prayers, by the parable of the Pharifee and Publican.

Prayer to God should be from the heart; and humbly performed, will ever be efficacious in preventing fin; becaufe it is an impoffibility for the man, who with a right faith addreffes the Almighty, to engage in any predetermined action, that will render him obnoxious to his fellow creatures.—'Tis not for man to judge who are the penitent finners; but the hypocrite may be affured, that his hypocrify cannot be concealed from God, nor defended from the punifhment which is juftly due to a mockery of the moft high, performed for the purpofe of deceiving man.

Our duty to ourfelves confifts in exercifing properly the faculties which the omnipotent has given us as rational Beings.

We perceive the exalted ftate in which we are placed upon this earth; yet we are fenfible of the infirmities of our nature :—but the defign of God in creation appears evidently to have proceeded from his defire of communicating happinefs :—Without affiftance from others, life lofes half its comforts, and the wants of our nature are beft relieved in fociety.—To affift others, in order that we may have a claim upon their affiftance, is a duty, that policy itfelf, without religion, will tell us ought not to be neglected ; but, in a religious fociety, where we are fatisfied that all our poffeffions come by the permiffion of God, it will appear indifpenfably our duty to relieve the wants of our fellow creatures.

Happinefs is the chief concern of our lives, and we may declare, that it is annexed to a ftrict performance of the will of God :—This we muft endeavour to accomplifh by properly ufing the powers which he has given us.

Our reafon, which we find capable of receiving not unworthy ideas of God's attributes, is fully able to direct us to the obtaining of whatfoever is neceffary for our exiftence ; but it requires cultivation to enable it to enjoy the full benefit of its powers. To improve our underftandings, in order to obtain a proper fenfe of the will of God, is therefore a very high duty.

In moft countries, prejudices and ignorance have fo overwhelmed the powers of reafon, that, even in the moft material articles of the happinefs of life, men

X

find themselves continually in an error; but they seem to take no advantage from experience.

God has created the human species male and female, as he has done the chief part of animated nature, and our births are regulated by similar laws. It will be seen, that even in this, which may be juftly esteemed so great a concern, God has not departed from his general laws; and that the birth of the first monarch upon earth is dependent upon similar circumstances with that of the meanest animal. — Nay, if man should be induced to abuse this prerogative of continuing his species, God has not, even in this, deprived him of his free agency.

The defire that is felt by all animals towards those of the contrary sex, leads them to continue their species; and God has implanted in all his creatures, such an affection for their young, as to prevent all wilful neglect.

The end being answered when the offspring is capable of taking care of itself, connubial ties are soon dissolved among the brute creation, and when a particular season is past, they generally live in solitude and separate tranquility, and new alliances are formed the next season.

In man, animal love rages with great power, and the wisdom of God directed that it should do so, foreseeing, that without it did, the race of man might become extinct, through the unpleasant situations into which his creature might, perhaps, bring himself, through misuse of his free agency.

But reason was made able to regulate this desire, and in those countries, where we are told a general dissoluteness takes place, it will be found to arise from the absurd ideas of the people, who foolishly endeavour to counteract the laws of nature.

There are some nations who esteem as virtuous, those who live single and have no connection with the other sex; but how ignorant must they be of the Creator, who suppose he is to be pleased with his creatures refraining from that which he has intended should be a means of accomplishing his will and of contributing to their happiness.

Continence, merely for continence sake, is far from being meritorious; it is really sinful, as being the determination to prevent the existence of beings, who might hereafter prove themselves worthy servants of their God.

Those nations talk of the virtue of avoiding temptations; of the necessity of punishing the flesh; and represent, as meritorious, many things which are evidently destructive of the designs of omnipotence.—But what is the result?—just as might be expected; for God's general laws are immutable, and are not to be broken without inconvenience.

As rational beings, who are advanced above the rest of the world, it becomes us to reflect seriously upon this matter:—Marriage is a concern of no small consequence to our happiness, and we ought thoroughly to acquaint ourselves with its nature and design.

When first born, man is perfectly feeble and helpless, and without the attentions of his parents, he would inevitably perish. Other animals become, in a short time, able to procure the necessaries of life, and to satisfy all their wants, but the infancy of man is long.

The brute creation receive from nature, with their strength, all the perfections which they are capable of using to their own advantage; but our reason requires cultivation ere it attains its powers; and without the assistance of others, we remain ignorant and weak: hence in mankind it is necessary, that family connections should be permanent, in order that children, by receiving the instructions of those who are naturally interested in their welfare, should attain the qualifications which, it becomes their duty to seek.

From not duly confidering thefe truths, many people complain of the ftraitnefs of the bands of marriage, and purfue the very means of rendering pofterity unhappy; for finding few comforts arife from their own imprudent conneftions, they conclude, that unhappinefs is more to be expefted than joy; and that, as marriage too often brings oppofite tempers into an indiffoluble union, other conveniencies are neceffary to render it defirable.

Yet, knowing the effeft of nature in youth, and confidering that fimilar want of experience may produce fimilar miftakes, they preach to their children, how likely their inexperience is to caufe them to fall into error, and defire them to put implicit faith in whatever they advife them.—And what is their advice?—Generally as follows:

As their children may fee from their own experience how few married couples are happy, they tell them, that they muft obferve how great is the danger of being unhappy in that ftate, and how foolifh it is to be attracted by perfonal qualifications; and fhewing them how liable they are to be deceived if they marry while young—defire them to take time to confider, to look out prudently, and when they do make their choice to take care to have fubftance to comfort them in cafe they fhould be miftaken; and fpeak of wealth as the only fure anchor to depend on.

Thus educated, a young man dares not fay to his parents, " fuch a woman is in pofleffion of every qualification of beauty and virtue that is to be found or defired in the fex, and I wifh to make her my wife, unlefs at the fame time he can fay that her fortune is likewife as defirable. Without fortune the choice will be difapproved of, and a reply will be made, " that there is no occafion to be in a hurry."

In thofe countries the refult is too often as follows: A young man finding his firft affections checked, his life becomes uncomfortable; his friends, as they efteem themfelves, endeavour to enliven him, by leading him into fcenes of gaiety and diffipation;—his parents, perhaps, wink at this as being in their opinion, the leaft error, and fuch a one as they think age and experience will correct; and they treat with the name of youthful follies, thofe actions which muft render the evening of his life uncomfortable:—when too late, they all find themfelves miftaken, and he labours under a bankrupt conftitution, with no other recompence than reflections that convince him of his folly.

But our legiflator wifely followed nature in all her directions, and endeavoured to ftrengthen the power of reafon. He faw that the paffion of love was not to be trifled with, and that the happinefs of community depended upon its being duly regulated, according to the dictates of reafon.

He thought that encouragement should be given to youth to marry prudently, and that inducements should be held out for parents to do their duty. He put marriage upon the footing of nature, and declared that cohabitation alone conſtituted it in the eyes of God; but wiſhed that every man and woman who choſe to cohabit, would ſubmit to the ceremony he had appointed, in order that due reſpect might be paid to all married people.

He ordained, that parents ſhould have no other controul over their children than what reaſon gave them; and has even prevented them from paſſionately depriving them of their ſhare in their fortune——And what has been the effect?—That there is now before me the moſt happy congregation in the world. — For parents, knowing the independence of their children, exert their affection ſolely from motives of procuring the true happineſs of their children:—and our youth, perceiving that parents have no other motives for the advice they give than to produce their real happineſs, and knowing, by their own reaſon, that every action is directed to that one end, expreſs that ſubmiſſion in every reſpect which other nations have fooliſhly attempted to force by laws, which tend to counteract the operations of nature.

Prevented from abuſing their truſts, parents themſelves have the natural inclination of providing for the welfare of their children, both ſtrengthened and duly regulated; and the advantage hereof is fully proved, by this nation finding the marriage state, as was intended by God, the fountain of happiness on earth.

In other countries the gift of God, whereby he permits us to become parents, is but little considered in the light it ought to be, and is too generally abused, to the destruction of the end intended.

Debaucheries are committed at a very early period of life, and the artificial forced state which the vices of those nations permit their youth to experience, soon debilitates and weakens their faculties.—Parents tenderly overlook many irregularities, till familiarized to vice by general depravity, they, with impotent concern, see their children follow a course which their own folly has occasioned; yet comfort themselves with the hope, that the error will be wiped away when the heat of youth is over.—Vain expectation! As numbers have experienced to their sorrow.

Our friend Jacobus, acquainted with the errors of other countries, endeavoured to provide against them, and knowing that human nature was every where the same, established such laws and regulations as he thought would produce happiness to his people.

Ignorance he believed to be the sole cause of mankind's committing sin; and every thing that human forefight could provide, to bring man from ignorance to the knowledge of his own nature, has been prepared by him.

By his regulations, was the chief concern of life, marriage, put upon that natural rational footing, of which we now reap the benefit; and our children are taught to look upon it, as it undoubtedly is, a matter of the greatest importance.

Free to chufe our companions; taught to felect them for their real worth; the numerous happy families which furround us, befpeak the virtues of their anceftors One principle actuates the whole; and joy and pleafure are confpicuous in every countenance.——The time that is not engaged in the neceffary bufinefs of life, is employed, by all, to the improvement of others.——Each perfon, in every family, is ftudious to gain and to difpenfe knowledge; and happinefs is ardently fought for and promoted.——The manly virtues are difcoverable in all our boys; temperance and fortitude is confpicuous in every countenance; while that blufhing delicacy of the female fex, which was formed as a lovely contraft to the neceffary hardinefs of man, is here difcovered in its fulleft perfection.——To my young friends, I shall now particularly addrefs myfelf.

Ye are, my beloved, attending here, through the love of God, to endeavour to render him acceptable fervice, to worship him; to thank him for the blessings ye have received; and, by the instructions here given you, to learn to know your duty, in order that ye may truly perform his will.

The knowledge of the true God is here taught you; your mental faculties are strengthened; your reasons are improved; and ye receive from your parents, every assistance which human nature requires.— -Ye must be sensible the obligations which ye owe to your parents, can never be repaid by you; and how inadequate all your returns must be, for the pains they have taken, in giving you your education: Exert therefore your endeavours, to render their lives happy and agreeable.

Obedience to their commands is at all times due, unless (which can hardly be) they are contrary to the commands of God.

The obedience I inculcate, is not an entire giving up of your reason and opinion to theirs: In all cases, exert your own, but examine with coolness, whether you are not wrong; for though your parents, as mortals, are liable to error, yet their experience enables them to judge properly of many things with which you are totally unacquainted.

If any different opinion arises in your minds, express it with openness; beg of your parents to give their reasons, why they differ from you, and intreat them to explain them to you; if not convinced, and should your parents enforce their opinions by commands, examine within your own breasts, what are likely to be the consequences; if they appear fatal to your future happiness, with humility decline to act, and wait till future events shall render every thing more clear.——There can little harm happen from avoiding action; and as ye increase in years, ye will perceive that the ideas of youth are often found by age, to be erroneous.——But when mere positive commands of immediate service, are the points which ye are tempted to contest, be ye assured, that it is a duty incumbent upon you, to shew your obedience, in the strictest sense of the word; nor ought the sacrifice of life itself to be objected to, if it should happen that by this only, your parents happiness could be preserved.

To parents who have done their duty, it is impossible to make an adequate return, and where this duty has been unfortunately neglected, it does not absolve children from the performance of theirs.— In all the reciprocal duties, the neglect of one party does not justify the failure of the other; for the obligation is in fact, to the Supreme. — And indeed there is more merit in the party who fulfills his duty, where the other fails, than where it is only an equal return.

Ye who are about to enter into life, have been taught by your parents how great a concern are the marriage engagements, and how neceſſary it is to chuſe virtuous companions,—Take the advice of a ſincere friend.

As ſoon as ye perceive within your breaſts a partiality for another, conſider whether your ſituation in life is ſuch as will permit you with honor to enter into the marriage ſtate.—Having ſatisfied yourſelves that ye will be juſtified in uniting yourſelves in marriage with the perſon whom ye love:—Search into their conduct towards their parents and their fellow creatures, and acquaint yourſelves with their virtues; if the examination proves favorable, apply to your parents for their advice, who may point out to your notice, many things of real conſequence, which your inexperience has prevented you from noticing.

Marriage is not a tranſient act, where an error may be committed and hereafter retrieved, No!—One miſtake is never to be recovered, and the reſt of your lives may be a perpetual ſtruggle between duty and ſorrow.

Let not precipitation be ſhewn in your conduct, but encourage, within your own breaſt, that high ſenſe of true honor, which will lead you to prove yourſelves entitled to the reſpect and friendſhip of all who know you; ſo ſhall the bleſſings of God be upon you, and happineſs ſhall be your reward.

And ye, my younger friends, let me intreat you to apply with affiduity, to the inftructions of your parents; feek to acquaint yourfelves with your own nature, and learn to know your God:——Thus employed, ye will difcover the obligations which ye owe to your parents, thro' God, for every bleffing ye enjoy; and ye will, I am perfuaded, purfue thofe means of affording them comfort, which your reafon fhall point out to you, as moft likely to fucceed.

Let not paffion, of any kind, remain within your breafts any longer than it is impoffible for you to avoid; try to command your tempers, and be careful at all times to regulate your behaviour; with fubmiffion and refpect to your fuperiors; with freedom and friendfhip to your equals; with meeknefs, complacency, and generofity to your inferiors.—We are all of the fame clafs of beings, but the Almighty has been pleafed to permit an inequallity of rank, which does not exalt the individual more than it exalts human nature. Hence are our employments divided;—the good of the community is attended to and increafed;—and each fills, with advantage to the whole, that particular occupation which his birth has allotted him.

Upon due government of your tempers, and proper attention in cultivating the faculties you poffefs, depends every hope that delights human nature.—While ignorance and bad difpofitions produce unhappinefs in every rank.

In the reciprocal return of kind offices, which a due performance of the duties of fociety produces in all parties, will be found that happinefs, which extends its effects even beyond the grave.—For confident in the mercies of God, confcious of having, to the utmoft of our abilities, fulfilled the duties of our nature, — our death bed will afford us fuch a profpect of happinefs as will diminifh all its terrors.

Thus, no time of life will be unprovided for Death; nor fhall we be uneafy at the certainty of it.——But continual refignation to the will of Omnipotence, whether in life or death, will mark us as Beings who love their Creator.——All our actions will be under the regulation of reafon: our mental faculties will be duly cultivated and improved; and when the time fhall arrive, that our bodies fhall go to the grave, our fouls will, with firmnefs declare, that there is but one Lord God omnipotent, the Creator of the World! Bleffed be his name, for ever and ever! Amen.

HAVING thus given a view of the chief of their religious principles, from their own writings, I shall now subjoin those general laws, with the remarks, &c. which are copied in all their churches: There are certain tables, around the walls, upon which all public acts are recorded, as well the particular regulations with respect to the single parish, these are altered according as circumstances may require; but the following are permanent, and not liable to any alteration: These last are engraved in stone, whereas the others are only painted.

L A W S.

Thou shalt have none other Gods but one.

Remarks. Convinced as we are, that there is a God, and that he is a sole self-existent Being; we cannot suffer any foriegner to become entitled to the previleges of our Citizens, but such as prove, by their actions, their firm belief in God, which, only can make them good members of society.——And in case any Foreigner wishes to be admitted into our society, he must pass two years of probation, and then, upon the hundred court giving testimonials of his virtue to parliament, he shall be entitled to a naturalization act. But let him reflect, that the morals of our society are strictly guarded, and we cannot suffer any one to corrupt them; we believe that the soul will be entitled to future happiness, either from having pursued a course of virtue, or, perhaps, by repentance of former sins, with a due restitution made for them. Let not the Foreigner attempt, from improper or hypocritical motives, to join in our community; he cannot deceive God, he will hardly deceive us: If he offends wilfully against any of our laws; the courts are authorized to inflict double punishments, and afterwards to expell him from the society.

If any of our subjects deny the truth of this law, not being strictly an idiot, let him be taken before the parish court, who must examine carefully into the charge; and upon sufficient proof, let the court send him to solitary confinement, where he may be fed sparingly, for one month; let him be supplied with books, containing the opinions of different nations upon this subject; let him be desired to read them, and to satisfy his mind whether there is a God or not; let the parish minister frequently attend him, and lead him to a proper observation of the wonderful harmony displayed through all creation.—If after the month is expired, he should still continue in ignorance, let him be sent back for another month, and be left entirely by himself, but furnished with every book which he may wish to examine; should he still be in doubt, whether there is a God, let him be brought before the hundred court, which if convinced that he is neither an idiot nor a lunatic, shall banish him out of the kingdom for ever.

The reason is; because any man who denies that there is a God, must be either unfortunately ignorant, or else very wicked—If the first, his ignorance should be done away; if the latter, he is not fit for ou society; but as the experience which he may gain by being obliged to see the works of God in other countries may either amend or convince him, we are bound to give him every chance.

L A W.

Thou shalt not take the name of the Lord thy God in vain.

When the Lord's name is used, it should be with the highest veneration and respect, and every person must perceive how great an offence it is to join a falsity with it.

If any man is proved before the hundred court to have sworn falsely, or borne false witness, let him be committed to solitary confinement for three months, for the first offence; for two years, for the second offence; and for the rest of his life, for the third conviction.

Remarks.—These offences proceed from ignorance, and it is a duty in the state to endeavour to call its subjects to the use of their reason. But if a man is three times convicted of perjury, there are but few hopes of his amendment by letting him remain among his fellow creatures; therefore solitude will prevent him from doing any mischief, and may call him to a knowledge and repentance of his sin.

LAW.

Thou shalt not steal.

This relates to injuries done to the property of others, and reparation shall be made two-fold. But when the court shall think the offence requires further punishment it shall order the culprit into solitary confinement, for not longer than two months, unless by order of council, upon an application from the hundred court.

LAW.

Thou shalt not commit adultery.

God having made the human race, as well as the other animals, male and female; and having ordained that the early period of our lives should be particularly feeble, and in want of the protection of our parents, it becomes necessary for the welfare of community, that proper care be taken by the state to preserve inviolate the honourable connection of matrimony.

Marriage consists in the union of two persons of different sexes, whereby they give to each other an undivided property in themselves. The good of the world requires that these connections should never be broken.

Adultery consists in wilfully breaking a first connection by living in the same intimacy with another while the first choice is still existing.

Both the parties convicted of adultery shall be committed to perpetual solitary confinement, which will oblige them to reflect on their sin, and by inducing repentance, may enable them to obtain the forgiveness of Omnipotence. When sentence is passed the marriage is *ipso facto* dissolved, and the free person is at liberty at the end of six months to marry again.

LAW.

Thou shalt do no murder.

The man who has committed wilful murder has proved himself an improper person to be permitted to remain in society, and has committed an injury which he can never repair. From God alone can he receive absolution, which can only be obtained by that sincere repentance and contrition, which a true sense of the henioufness of the offence, together with a belief in the mercies of God can only effect.

The murderer shall suffer amputation of his right hand; and be chained to the ground for the rest of his days in solitary confinement; let him be furnished with such books as may serve to call him to a sense of the injury he has committed. Let him see nobody but the goaler, and the minister of the parish, who is requested occasionally to visit him, and to assist him with such advice as may enable him, if possible, to make his peace with God.

In most other countries, murder is punished with death, but the spirit of our laws is not to punish, but to amend. We do not think we have any right to kill; because we cannot say whether God will accept death as an expiation; but we do hope, that upon a sincere repentance, he will pardon—and this effect may be produced through solitude and self-examination.

LAW.

Thou shalt not injure thy neighbour in any of his possessions.

All injuries shall be repaired two-fold. Where this cannot be done, the offender shall be sent to prison for a certain time according to the opinion of the court, having respect to the extent of his offences.

Every magistrate has the power of sending any offender to prison till the setting of the next parish court; where the offence must be investigated, and the punishment declared. If any perfon knows himfelf injured he may appeal in the following order:

FROM THE PARISH COURT,
TO
THE HUNDRED;
TO
THE KING IN COUNCIL;
AND TO
THE PARLIAMENT.

But to prevent troublefome appeals, it is ordained that any fuperior court confirming the fentence of an inferior, fhall be at liberty to double the penalty.

If any magiftrate acts malicioufly, upon application to the Chancellor's Court, the injured will meet with redrefs.

F I N I S.

I Shall, perhaps, make another trip to Veritas before I come to England; if I do, I will acquaint myself with some further particulars of the customs of this island, of which I know you will be glad to be informed

I am,

Your sincere Friend,

J. RICHARDSON.

ERRATA.

Page 2,—Line 8—read Genius
  3————12————Supreme
  ————20————Of the King and Parliament
  9————12————were obliged
  25————————The Te Deum ought to have preceded the Litany
  54 ——laſt line——Civil Ceremonies
  62——laſt line———ſhould be to reflect
  76————21————add a Comma after, with it
  91————16————in ſhort he alone, and dele the word alone in the next line
  105————9————yet they believe that
  109————16————divine aid
  114————10————general
  121————2————dele but
  126————18————had given
  128————7————the Feaſts
  133————13————a fair Statement

www.ingramcontent.com/pod-product-compliance
Lightning Source LLC
Chambersburg PA
CBHW020247170426
43202CB00008B/260